TOURING IN WINE COUNTRY

BORDEAUX

MITCHELL BEAZLEY

TOURING IN WINE COUNTRY
BORDEAUX

HUBRECHT DUIJKER

SERIES EDITOR
HUGH JOHNSON

Contents

**Touring in Wine Country
Bordeaux**
by Hubrecht Duijker

First published in Great Britain in 1996
by Mitchell Beazley, an imprint of
Octopus Publishing Group Limited,
2–4 Heron Quays, London E14 4JP

Reprinted 1997
Revised edition 2000
Reprinted 2000

Copyright © Octopus Publishing Group
Ltd 1996, 1997, 2000
Text copyright © Hubrecht Duijker
1996, 1997, 2000
Maps copyright © Octopus Publishing
Group Ltd 1996, 1997, 2000

Text adapted in part from 'Bordeaux – A
Wine Lover's Touring Guide' by Hubrecht
Duijker. First published 1993 by
Uitgeverij Het Spectrum BV

A CIP catalogue record of this book is
available from the British Library

ISBN 1 84000 246 8

Editors: Susan Keevil, Lucy Bridgers,
Hilary Lumsden
Art Editor: Paul Drayson
Senior Art Editor: Susan Downing
Index: Angie Hipkin
Gazetteer: Sally Chorley
Production: Juliette Butler
Managing Editor: Sue Jamieson
Art Director: Gaye Allen
Cartography: Map Creation Limited
Design by Bridgewater Book Company
Illustrations: Polly Raines

Typeset in Bembo and Gill Sans

Printed and bound in by Toppan Printing
Company

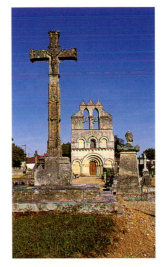

Foreword

Why is it that wine tasted in the cellar (or even in the region) of its birth has a magic, a vibrancy and vigour that makes it so memorable?

It is easy to think of physical reasons. The long journey to the supermarket shelf cannot be without some effect on a living creature – and wine is indeed alive, and correspondingly fragile.

It is even easier to think of romantic reasons: the power of association, the atmosphere and scents of the cellar, the enthusiasm of the grower as he moves from barrel to barrel...

No wonder wine touring is the first-choice holiday for so many people. It is incomparably the best way to understand wine whether at the simple level of its scenery and culture, or deeper into the subtleties of its *terroirs* and the different philosophies of different producers.

There are armchair wine books, coffee-table books, quick-reference wine books... even a pop-up wine book. Now with this series we have the wine-traveller's precise, pin-pointed practical guide to sleuthing through the regions that have most to offer, finding favourites and building up memories. The bottles you find yourself have the genie of experience in them.

Hugh Johnson

A First Acquaintance

The name Bordeaux has several applications: it is a city, a region, a wine, even a particular way of growing and making that wine. Bordeaux is, justifiably, the world's premier wine city. It has always led with regard to quality. This was already evident in 1855 with the first official classification of the Médoc and Sauternes *grands crus classés* châteaux. It was Bordeaux that established a worldwide reputation for practically all aspects of scientific research into wine through its oenological institute. Not only this, but *barriques* – the 225-litre casks used worldwide for ageing wine – originated in Bordeaux. The region's traditional grape varieties are used throughout the world to improve the quality of local wines. And it is due to Bordeaux that the word 'château' has become an honorary accolade. In short, Bordeaux is a phenomenon.

The city of Bordeaux is the sixth-largest in France, and is the centre of the most renowned wine region in the world. Bordeaux lies on the Garonne River, which joins the Dordogne at Bourg just north of the city. From this confluence the waterway is called the Gironde. It flows into the Atlantic between Le Verdon, at the most northerly point of the Médoc, and the town of Royan. The Médoc, Blaye and Bourg wine districts lie either side of the Gironde estuary.

The presence of these rivers is of the utmost importance for winegrowing, as the water serves to regulate air temperatures surrounding the vines. In the past they were also important as a means of transport. In many ways, the development of the wine trade here is due to the rivers, and access to the open sea. The Atlantic Ocean makes itself felt in the rivers, for the ebb and flow of the tides is perceptible above Bordeaux and Libourne.

Left The imposing entrance to Château Beychevelle in the commune of St-Julien. This fourth-growth château has long been popular with the British, and its wines are in demand worldwide.

Right Neat, straight rows of vineyards dominate the landscape of Bordeaux.

CLIMATE

The people in Paris are emphatic that Bordeaux has the best climate in France and this may well be true. Although the influence of the seasons is clearly observable, the climate is generally mild: the average winter temperature is 7.5°C; in summer it is 18°C. Hard frosts only happen occasionally but they can do considerable damage to the vines. In April 1991 night-time temperatures dropped to -11°C causing devastation in the vineyards. Those close to the River Gironde were the least affected, thanks to its moderating influence.

There is certainly no lack of sun in Bordeaux; the average is 2,010 hours of sunshine per year, giving plenty of dry, warm weather for ripening the grapes. The not uncommon Indian summers are also beneficial. They say in Bordeaux '*Bel automne vient plus souvent que beau printemps*', and it is true that spring here can be fresh and damp, while autumn is often sunny. Such a climate is one of the most important factors behind Bordeaux's high quality.

SIGHTS TO SEE

Bordeaux's countryside is particularly appealing. Not only are the city and winegrowing districts well worth seeing, but so, too, is the coastal strip along the Atlantic. Dozens of miles of sandy beaches spread along the coast. Behind them, romantic lakes, conifer woods (Les Landes forest is the biggest in Europe), resorts and harbours await discovery. In summer you can engage in practically any outdoor sport.

Lacanau is one of the coastal resorts – with a golf school and a fine golf course. Others well-known are Soulac, Montalivet,

Bordeaux

– · – · –	Département boundary
▬▬▬	Limit of Appellation Bordeaux
▢	Haut-Médoc/St-Emilion
▢	Médoc/Pomerol
▢	Canon-Fronsac/St-Emilion
▢	Fronsac/Bordeaux et Entre-Deux-Mers-Haut-Benauge
▢	Côtes de Castillon
▢	Lalande-de-Pomerol/Côtes de Francs
▢	Blayais
▢	Pessac-Léognan

▢	Bourgeais
▢	Premières Côtes de Bordeaux
▢	Graves de Vayres
▢	Ste-Foy-Bordeaux/Côtes de Bordeaux-St-Macaire
▢	Graves
▢	Cérons
▢	Sauternes and Barsac
▢	Loupiac
▢	Ste-Croix-du-Mont/Entre-Deux-Mers

BOURG • Principal wine commune

[28] Area mapped at larger scale on page shown

1:570,000

Km. 0 5 10 15 20 25 Km.
Miles 0 5 10 15 Miles

glisottes-
-laures
Christophe-
Double

188-

N

STE-FOY-LA-GRANDE D936 Dordogne
ts-et-
-rtin Eynesse St-André-
ls Gensac et-Appelles
St-Quentin-
de-Caplong Margueron
Pellegrue
Cazaugitat Côtes de
Duras
Dieulivol
Monségur
Roquebrune St-Vivien-
de-Monségur
Réole
tet
Agen

Hourtain and Maubuisson, all tucked away among the never-ending coniferous woods. It would be wrong to suppose that these woods are ancient, as none of them was planted until the 19th century. Before this, Les Landes was a boggy, almost inaccessible area where the inhabitants had to walk about on stilts in winter. Fortunately those days are long gone, and the conifers are now an important source of timber. All the railway lines laid down after World War I to transport logs for the timber trade have since been converted into cycleways, of which there are now several hundred kilometres.

The Bassin d'Arcachon is another well-loved location. Home to an important nature reserve and many oyster farms, it looks like a lake but has an outlet to the ocean. Famous places here include Arcachon itself – where many well-to-do Bordeaux winegrowers have apartments or second homes around the Bassin – the Gujan-Mestras, Cap Ferret, and Andernos.

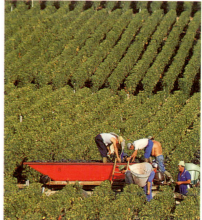

Top *Working the vineyards at Château d'Yquem.*
Above *The harvest at Châteaux Cos d'Estournel and* (right) *Lafite.*

12

Arcachon is a pleasant resort with its own distinctive aura. A strong period atmosphere prevails, so that at times you almost think yourself back in the 1920s. There is a pier from which boat trips out on the Bassin are run. To the south of Arcachon lies Pyla, with the highest sand-dune in Europe. Climbing it you might imagine yourself crossing the Sahara but, at the top, you look out over Arcachon and the Atlantic.

You can get to Arcachon from Bordeaux by the motorway that leads to Bayonne, or by the N250, leaving the ring road at Pessac. The former is quicker. You need to allow more time for the N250, but the advantage is that it takes you to Gujan-Mestras and La Teste – where there is a large bird park and a butterfly garden. Although every little harbour around the Bassin has *cabanes* selling oysters, these are very much the speciality of Gujan-Mestras. There are also some excellent fish restaurants and an important oyster festival.

The Bordeaux area is a paradise for lovers of golf. There are ten or so courses around the city where anyone may play. For walkers there are plenty of pathways in the pine forests and along the beaches. Those who like castles and abbeys will enjoy Entre-Deux-Mers; and for wine-lovers there are the viticultural districts and their many châteaux. All these attractions can be enjoyed within a radius of 50 to 80 kilometres of Bordeaux.

WINE ROUTES

The road most used for visiting the famous Médoc châteaux is the D2. This starts just outside Bordeaux. Take the Le Verdon direction turning off the ring road, then turn right towards Pauillac. It winds through the Médoc to Saint-Vivien, passing many of the renowned *grands crus classés* châteaux

(most of which are described in this guide). Another recommended wine route goes from Bordeaux via the right bank of the Garonne through the Premières Côtes de Bordeaux: Bordeaux, Latresne, Camblanes, Quinsac, Cambes, Baurech, Tabanac, Le Tourne, Langoiran, Haux, Saint-Caprais, Cenac, and back to Bordeaux. This journey of some 55 kilometres takes you through one of the loveliest areas of the Bordelais.

Signposting in the Sauternes, another district with its own wine route, is good and you can reach the area in less than half an hour from Bordeaux. This is a region famed for its idyllic and impressive estates.

For routes around Saint-Emilion, Graves and Entre-Deux-Mers, refer to the relevant chapters.

WINEGROWING AND WINES

The Bordeaux wine region covers about 115,000 hectares. This makes it five times as big as Burgundy and as extensive as all the vineyards of Germany or South Africa. Yet in the mid-19th century the total area was even greater. The decrease was due to devastation wrought by the phylloxera insect and the spread of towns and villages. Wine is of such great importance to Bordeaux, however, that almost 110,000 hectares of *appellation contrôlée* vineyards exist there.

All in all there are some 13,000 winegrowers, of which 5,000 belong to cooperatives, and there are 400 wine firms. Put into a more personal perspective, one in six people in the Gironde works with wine. Château vineyards average at about five hectares, but many are half this size, and very few exceed 20 hectares (75 per cent for red, 25 per cent for white). There are 53 *appellations contrôlées*, which cover red, dry white, sweet white, rosé, *clairet* (light red) and *crémant* (sparkling).

THE CLASSIFICATIONS

The 1800s in the Médoc saw most châteaux come into being and also the first official wine classification in 1855. Expertise was pooled to elevate 88 châteaux to *grand cru classé* status. Médoc *crus* were subdivided into three *premiers crus*, 15 *deuxièmes crus* (second growths), 14 *troisièmes*, ten *quatrièmes* and 18 *cinquièmes*. These categories are still used, along with '*cru bourgeois*' for the next level down. For Sauternes there was one *premier cru supérieur* (Château d'Yquem), 11 *premiers crus* and 15 *deuxièmes crus*. After World War II, two further

Top *Cabernet Sauvignon grapes give the wine backbone and tannin, not to mention the typical blackcurrant and cedarwood flavours.* Left *Merlot grapes are thinner-skinned than Cabernet and best suited to heavier, clay soils.* Above *Sémillon grapes which have been attacked by the highly desirable 'Noble Rot'; this dehydrates the grape, concentrating the grape sugars.*

classifications were created: that of Graves, with 15 *crus classés*, and Saint-Emilion, now with 63 *grands crus classés* and 11 *premiers grands crus classés* (two 'A's and nine 'B's).

GRAPE VARIETIES

Unlike the wines of other wine regions, such as Alsace and Burgundy, Bordeaux wines are almost always made from more than one variety. The properties of these grapes complement each other and, after vinification and the final blending a wine is obtained that is highly characteristic of its appellation. One Bordeaux wine will always be different from another.

The varieties used have remained practically unchanged since the Middle Ages. For red wine the grapes are: Merlot, Cabernet Sauvignon, Cabernet Franc, Malbec and Petit Verdot. For white: Sauvignon Blanc, Sémillon, Muscadelle, Colombard and Ugni Blanc. Differences between these varieties are substantial. Cabernet Sauvignon, for instance, is harvested later than Merlot, so has longer to ripen and can often benefit from warm weather in October. Broadly speaking, Merlot could be said to give suppleness to its wine, whereas Cabernet Sauvignon lends more backbone, and tannin. A useful insight into Bordeaux style comes from the fact that Cabernet predominates in the Médoc, while Saint-Emilion and Pomerol are largely Merlot's domain. Malbec and Petit Verdot had disappeared from the scene to some extent but, thanks to current oenological thinking, they seem to be making a comeback. However, they usually represent no more than 2 to 3 per cent of the grapes grown – although there may be more Malbec in Côtes de Bourg and Blaye, even as much as 30 per cent.

The difference between the white varieties Sauvignon and Sémillon is greater than that between Cabernet and Merlot. Sauvignon gives fresh, fragrant lively wines; Sémillon wines are more rounded, supple and powerful. Sweet wines are made from both. Other whites are somewhat simpler in style.

SOIL

A mild climate and high-quality grapes would be of little significance without good soil. Soils of various compositions occur in the Gironde. This is one of the reasons for the differences between the wines. Many layers of soil were brought down by the rivers in primeval times, notably gravels from the Pyrenees, the Massif Central and other upland areas. Various kinds of gravel became mixed together, and, in certain places, deep accumulations occurred. These 'croupes' offer an excellent and varied medium and perfect drainage for vine roots. The Médoc has many of these gravel hills, and they also occur in the Graves and Saint-Emilion.

In other parts of Bordeaux the vines are hardly less well-off on soils of limestone, clay, sand, or mixtures of these. The limestone slopes of Saint-Emilion and the clay plateau of Pomerol show that great wines can come from other soils, too.

THE HUMAN FACTOR

Finally there is the human factor, without which good wine could never be produced. The unremitting toil of the winegrower is of the utmost importance for achieving good quality. The grower is busy the whole year through with wine and vine, in the vineyard or in the *chais*. He, or she, determines the ultimate quality by deciding on the moment for picking, the choice of grapes, the method of wine fermentation, and the treatment of the wine.

THE CUISINE

Wine and gastronomy go together: wine is made to accompany the courses and enhance the content of a meal. In Bordeaux there is an added dimension in the presence of the châteaux. For many wine-lovers, being invited to a meal at a château is an honour and a festive occasion.

The owners do not always live in their châteaux, but they like receiving guests there. Not so long ago, you could make an appointment for a tasting and be automatically invited for lunch; but alas, those days are gone. The keynote of such a meal is usually the traditional regional cuisine: duck's liver (*foie gras de canard*), grilled *entrecôtes* or lamb, cheese and dessert are frequently served. The food always tastes good,

Main picture and above right
*Bordeaux is renowned for its
wonderful fresh seafood which goes so
well with Entre-Deux-Mers wines.*

*Food shopping in and around
Bordeaux is excellent for anything
from bread (above left) to specialities
such as charcuterie (below).*

and there is the privilege of being able to drink the wines of
several vintages from the château in question. A meal like
this remains a unique event, and is guaranteed to show off
the wine at its very best.

As to dishes, the regional cuisine of Bordeaux has much
to offer. There is lamb from Pauillac; oysters from the Bassin
d'Arcachon (often eaten with a *crépinette*, a small sausage);
duck, and the specialities derived from it, from neighbouring
Gers; asparagus from Blaye; beef (*blonde d'Aquitaine*) from
Bazas; sea fish, crustaceans and shellfish from the Atlantic;
sausages (*boudins*) from Lormont; lamprey and white
shrimps from the Gironde; the sweet *canalés* from Bordeaux;
and Saint-Emilion macaroons. It could be said that all that
is lacking is a local cheese. The Bordelais reply that they are
happy to avail themselves of farm cheese from Holland,
which they describe as 'the other cheese country'.

Worthy of separate mention is the *entrecôte, grillée aux
sarments de vigne* – sirloin (or rib of beef, or lamb cutlets)
grilled over smouldering vine twigs. Even the very greatest
red wines show to full advantage with this country dish. It
is also one of the traditional meals served to grape-pickers
during the harvest – quite often as a breakfast. Very special,
too, is lamprey in a red-wine sauce, *lamproie à la Bordelaise*.
This curious, elongated predatory fish still frequents the
Gironde, where it may be caught in limited numbers in
the spring. Lampreys are usually potted and may be bought
in Kilner-type jars from delicatessens or *traiteurs*. They
are said to gain flavour with time in bottle.

After a long absence the sturgeon is back in the Gironde
– and so is caviar. Visit L'Esturgeonnière, Route de Mios-
Balanos in Le Teich; *telephone: 05 56 22 69 50*. White, almost
transparent shrimps known as *chevrettes* are another speciality.
These are eaten with aperitifs and can be bought in the
guinguettes (country taverns) along the rivers.

How to Use this Guide

In words and pictures this guide takes you through practically all the wine districts of Bordeaux, regarded as the biggest quality wine-producing region in the world. For each wine town or village the most important things to see are carefully reported. In Saint-Emilion, for example, the book will guide you around the most notable monuments, and pick out other items of interest, such as shops where you can buy regional delicacies.

Outside the larger communities, Bordeaux has only a modest number of good hotels. This is why in some places an address for *chambres d'hôte* (accommodation in private rooms) is given. Restaurants are listed, including some very simple and affordable ones. Some of the places to stay and places to eat are not to be found in any other guide which does not imply that spending time in them is unpleasant. The hotel prices given usually refer to double rooms without breakfast. Restaurant prices represent the cheapest set menus, without drinks.

The best winemakers for each district are listed, too. This is a very modest selection of all the châteaux and cooperatives in Bordeaux, but it amounts to hundreds nevertheless.

HOTEL RESERVATIONS

When making a hotel reservation always ask for a quiet room at the back, or facing the courtyard if there is one. Look out for any nearby church bells likely to ring loudly and often. When reserving a room you will usually be given a latest time to book in. Should you be thinking of arriving later, ring up on the day to let the hotel know, otherwise there is a chance you will lose your room. Written confirmation of your reservation may be prudent. Do this by letter or by fax. Lists of private persons who rent out rooms (*gîtes* or *chambres d'hôte*) are usually kept at the town hall or its equivalent, or at the *office du tourisme*.

RESTAURANTS – EATING OUT IN BORDEAUX

Telephoning a restaurant in advance is recommended: both to be sure of a table and to check that it is open that day. It generally makes sense to order set menus: not only are prices relatively low, but their ingredients will often be fresh from the market. In the simpler eating houses it is usually best to choose regional dishes, as complicated recipes from elsewhere may overtax the chef. Always aim to choose the regional wines, preferably from the district you are in. These will have been selected more expertly and critically than wines from other appellations – let alone those from areas outside Bordeaux. A carafe of water is always free, and mineral waters can be ordered.

MEETING THE GROWERS AND VISITING THE CHATEAUX

It may take a good deal of effort to get to see the famous growers, particularly if they have no problems in selling their wines at high prices. There are quite a few wine-producing châteaux where it is made clear that visitors are not wanted. Do not give up too quickly, however, for if you are truly interested in wine, and make this apparent, most doors will be open to you. (Showing this guide may help: anyone who arrives thus recommended will usually have a friendlier reception than some-one who drops in casually.)

When tasting wines it is quite customary to spit them out, but ask first where you can do this. Ask, too, what you should do with any drops left in the glass; sometimes the producer has a special container for these. And never tip winegrowers; but buy, if you can, at least one bottle from them as a token of appreciation for the hospitality enjoyed. Generally, French will be the only medium of communication, although many young winegrowers speak English nowadays.

THE CITY OF BORDEAUX

WINE SHOPS

Badie
62 Allées de Tourny; T: 05 56 52 23 72
Bordeaux Magnum
3 Rue Gobineau; T: 05 56 48 00 06
Cousin et cie
Place du Parlement; T: 05 56 01 20 23
L'Intendant
2 Allées de Tourny; T: 05 56 48 01 29
L'Oenothèque de Bordeaux
1 Place du Chapelet; T: 05 56 52 01 66
La Vinothèque de Bordeaux
8 Cours du 30 Juillet; T: 05 56 77 52 32

HOTELS

Burdigala
116 Rue Georges Bonnat,
T: 05 56 90 16 16, F: 05 56 93 15 06
Ideally situated in the centre, with
spacious, nicely decorated rooms. Prices
around FF1,000; suites from FF1,500.
Château Chartrons Mercure
81 Cours Saint-Louis;
T: 05 56 43 15 00
Fine hotel, but you need transport into
the centre. Prices from FF700.

Main picture *The Fontaine
des Trois Graces in the Place de
la Bourse.*
Above right *The dramatic spire
of the Eglise St-Michel.*
Above *One of the numerous cafés
in the centre of Bordeaux, ideal for
either sampling some of the region's
wide variety of wines or simply
watching the world go by.*

The City of Bordeaux

Bordeaux is the most important economic centre in southwest France. Despite all the activity this entails, it is no longer so significant in its traditional role as a port. The Bordeaux quaysides are still a powerful tourist attraction and, quite often, cruise ships tie up opposite the beautiful Place de la Bourse. As a result of the reduced shipping trade, however, many dockside sheds now stand empty. If these often dilapidated buildings were to be pulled down, the Quai des Chartrons might regain its former lustre, for it is here that most of the wine merchants were originally established. A good deal of restoration work has already been done and many frontages have been cleaned. In addition, the opening of Bordeaux's southern ring road has put a stop to much of the heavy freight traffic.

Wine is especially important for the Bordeaux economy, but there are also other sources of income, including agriculture and industry (aviation, ship building, oil, chemicals, metals and space technology). The city is becoming

increasingly popular as a conference and exhibition centre. Just outside Bordeaux some vast exhibition halls have been built. Vinexpo, the world's biggest wine fair, is held in these halls every other year.

THE ARCHITECTURE

Many people visiting Bordeaux for the first time compare it to Paris. Part of the city is characterised by 18th-century buildings, broad avenues and boulevards (here called *allées*) in a similar style. Alternatively, French author Victor Hugo wrote 'Take Versailles, add Antwerp and you have Bordeaux'. Such comparisons hold far less weight today. Bordeaux has been afflicted by urban development – making it possible, for instance, for a contemporary shopping and office complex called the Mériadeck to be built right next to La Chartreuse, one of France's most splendid 19th-century town cemeteries. Evenings are now dark and forebodingly quiet in both.

Nevertheless, Bordeaux does have much that is beautiful to offer, including the Place de la Bourse, the Allées de Tourny (once a vineyard) where the striking Maison du Vin stands, and the Grand Théâtre nearby (built by Victor Louis, architect of the Paris Opéra). And no description of Bordeaux can leave out the Place (or

Claret
Cité Mondiale
T: 05 56 01 79 79, F: 05 56 01 79 00
By the quayside and in the old district of Chartrons. Prices around FF600.

Grand Hôtel Français
12 Rue Temple
T: 05 56 48 10 35, F: 05 56 81 76 18
Centrally located with comfortable, quiet rooms. Prices from about FF450.

Normandie
7 Cours du 30 Juillet
T: 05 56 52 16 80, F: 05 56 81 76 18
Classic hotel beside the Maison du Vin. Prices from about FF350.

Royal Médoc
5 Rue Sère
T: 05 56 81 72 42, F: 05 56 51 72 98
Hotel with good atmosphere and an agreeable bar. Prices around FF300.

Esplanade) des Quinconces: a remarkable raised urban 'plateau'. Here various events are organised, from fairs and *Quatorze Juillet* celebrations, to antique and flower markets. Also impressive are the great fountain monument to the Girondists and the Place du Parlement, which has almost a village character.

The old heart of the city, *le vieux Bordeaux*, is quietly being restored; you will find more and more art galleries setting up, unexpected, curious little shops and places to eat. If a structure is demolished, the city's antiquities service is on hand to carry out archaeological investigations before any new building is established. Thanks to this, more and more details of Roman life are coming to light and these are rarely better illustrated than by the Palais Gallien with its remains of a 3rd-century Roman amphitheatre. At the opposite extreme, the Cité Mondiale du Vin et des Spiritueux on the Quai des Chartrons (not far from the Place des Quinconces) is totally new. It is an imposing office block of stainless steel and glass, intended as a trade centre for wines and spirits. There are showrooms with wines from all over the world and

Top A traditional street sign for one of Bordeaux's many food shops. Above The bustling Rue Ste-Catherine in the centre of the city. Right Sunset over le Pont de Pierre Lampadaires.

 RESTAURANTS

Baud et Millet
19 Rue Hugurie
T: 05 56 79 05 77
Restaurant and a shop for wine and cheese. Many non-French wines and a lot of cheese. Set menus from FF120.

Le Bistro du Sommelier
167 Rue Georges Bonnac
T: 05 56 96 71 78
Owner is a well-known cellarman. Fascinating list of good *grands crus classés* for less than FF150 a bottle; many great names sold by the glass. Tasty set menu from around FF150.

La Chamade
20 Rue des Piliers-de-Tutelle
T: 05 56 48 13 74
Here, below the 18th-century arches, is one of Bordeaux's best restaurants. Set menus from FF180, and wines from all over Bordeaux.

Le Chapon Fin
5 Rue Montesquieux
T: 05 56 79 10 10
One of the best restaurants in

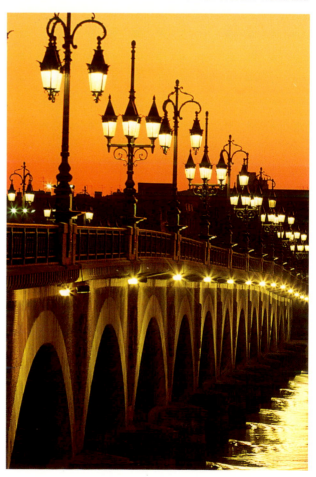

monthly, wine-themed exhibitions. In its hall a remarkable wall made up of bottles, reflects all the wine colours.

SHOPS AND MARKETS

Shopping in Bordeaux calls for some discernment. The Rue Sainte-Cathérine is one of the best spots. The 1,100-metres long street is packed with department stores and specialist shops. Ample parking space is available nearby, close to the

Place des Quinconces and below the Allées de Tourny. Modern shopping centres are the Mériadeck located in the city, featuring a covered car park, and the Bordeaux-Lac or Mérignac, by the airport. In the centre of Bordeaux there is the relatively new (and expensive) Les Grands Hommes: a handsome building with shops on three storeys and a car park below. The name is derived from the original Grands Hommes daily market held in the Allées de Tourny.

Anyone who loves markets should visit the Marché des Capuchins. From 5am you can buy fresh produce here in the company of Bordeaux's great chefs. This lies in the oldest quarter, near the Place de la Victoire, 'the belly of Bordeaux'. For the best chocolate, the Bordelais go to Saunion, a shop at 56 Cours Georges-Clémenceau, where three generations of craftsmanship provide marvellous confectionery. For the best cheese, go to Jean d'Alose in Rue Montesquieu. The shop at 25 Rue Camille-Sauvageau is tasteful, pleasant and Flemish, and belongs to Jan Demaitre, a true baker.

Top Elegant architecture dominates Bordeaux's centre.
Above Fresh local produce on sale at one of the city's markets.

southwest France; owner Francis Garcia is a great culinary figure in Bordeaux. Luxuriously furnished. Set lunch menus around FF170, with others up to about FF550. Excellent wine list with many affordable items.

Le Noailles
12 Allées de Tourny
T: 05 56 81 94 45
Prototype of a good Parisian-style brasserie: full, savoury, honest cooking, nice wines, relaxed atmosphere.

Didier Gélineau
26 Rue de Pas-Saint-Georges
T: 05 56 52 84 25
A place to spend time; attractive prices. Set menus from FF130.

Pavillon des Boulevards
120 Rue de la Croix-de-Seguey,
T: 05 56 81 51 02
Quite expensive but good. Modern-classic cuisine. Menus from FF400.

Chez Philippe
1 Place Parlement
T: 05 56 81 83 15
One of the very best places to go for fish, shellfish, crab and lobster. An interesting set menu at about FF200, but offering a choice of four starters, four main courses and four desserts.

Les Plaisirs d'Ausone
10 Rue Ausone
T: 05 56 79 30 30
Owner Michel Gauffine is a creative chef who constantly surprises his guests. Impressive wine list.

La Tupina
6 Rue Porte de la Monnaie
T: 05 56 91 56 37
One of the most original cuisines in Bordeaux, under the management of the dynamic and inventive Jean-Pierre Xiradakis. A sumptuous, nostalgic atmosphere, regional specialities and a very good list with affordable wines. Set menus from about FF150. Very good service.

BUYING WINE

Anyone going to the Bordeaux region who wants to buy wine, even if only to be able to say it was actually purchased there, has several options: directly from a château, at specialist shops, or from a hypermarket. Most of the *grands crus classés* châteaux do not sell 'on the premises', but many *crus bourgeois* do – although prices are no more favourable. Buying in a shop has the advantage that you can make comparisons. For a long time, the most obvious shop to do this was La Vinothèque, directly opposite the Maison du Vin. Other outlets include Badie, Bordeaux Magnum, and L'Intendant. Badie is an old-established name in Bordeaux. Bordeaux Magnum, at the back of the Maison du Vin, is a bright, fully air-conditioned place with a large selection, the emphasis being on wines from the Pessac and Léognan districts of Graves; it even has a branch in Tokyo. L'Intendant is a spectacular place to browse through a selection of bottles: visitors are guided down spiral stairs, the vintages getting older as you descend. In addition, there is a branch of Nicolas in the Cité Mondiale.

But, one of the nicest places to taste and buy Bordeaux wine is at Cousin & Cie, located behind the Place de la Bourse. Plus L'Oenothèque de Bordeaux is recommended offering more than 500 châteaux at competitive prices and also gives tastings and advice.

A good tip, however, is to buy your wine at a supermarket. Knowing that 60 per cent of the French public do just this could well be an extra incentive. Leclerc-Candéran and Leclerc-Léognan have a good-to-excellent choice of wine. Leclerc-Léognan is reputed to have the largest wine department in France.

Far left (top) *Part of the Monument des Girondins, celebrating Bordeaux's commercial importance in the early 19th century.* Far left (bottom) *Bordeaux is a haven for lovers of fish and seafood.* Left *Another of Bordeaux's markets, here, in front of the medieval town gate.*

Le Vieux Bordeaux
27 Rue Buhan
T: 05 56 52 94 36
In the heart of old Bordeaux is this atmospheric restaurant with brass candlesticks and red plush chairs. For years now there has been an excellent price-to-quality relationship. Set menus from around FF180. A substantial wine list with many great names.

RESTAURANTS: BORDEAUX AREA

ARCACHON
Chez Yvette
59 boulevard Général Leclerc,
T: 05 56 83 05 11
The best-known restaurant here with all the good things from the Bassin and the sea. Madame Yvette's fish soup is a speciality. Set menus around FF85.

ARES
St-Eloi
T: 05 56 60 20 46, F: 05 56 60 10 37
Near the water and the best place to eat on the north side of the Bassin. Classic regional, honest-to-goodness cooking. Set menus from about FF110. Also, hotel rooms from FF160.

GUJAN-MESTRAS
La Guérinière
T: 05 56 66 08 78, F: 05 56 66 13 39
Splendid hotel/restaurant with a friendly bar and a swimming pool. Good classic cuisine. Set menus from around FF150. Modern, comfortable rooms with terrace from FF460.
Les Viviers
T: 05 56 66 01 04
The Castaings have been a family of oyster farmers and restaurateurs for five generations. Their fish restaurant is uniquely situated on the harbour. Set menu from about FF130 from 12 noon; specialities of the day written on a board. Oysters here are marvellous; the fish dishes delicious and classic: *Plateau de fruits de mer* (around FF130) is the speciality. The simple, straightforward wine list is well attuned to the fish dishes served.

HOTELS

Ten years ago, hotel accommodation was rather scarce and disappointing for a city of this size. But, the picture has changed totally. Familiar hotel chains are now all present, and for tourists passing through, the Formule 1 hotels are popular as you only pay about FF180 for a room for three. In the centre of the city, there is now ample choice. The hotels Normandie and Royal Médoc are pleasant, somewhat old-fashioned and well situated. But Bordeaux's best option is probably the Burdigala – very comfortable and expensive. Alternatively, for those keen to immerse themselves fully in the world of wine, the luxurious Château Chartrons or the Claret Hotel in the Cité Mondiale are good choices.

RESTAURANTS

Eating out in this city is a great pleasure, for there are places to dine in all price categories. From 12.30pm it is often difficult to get a free table in any well-known establishment, but one of the attractions of lunch is that set menus may be lower in price than in the evenings. When there are so many restaurants, any recommendation has limited validity, but there is an abundance of good and often delightful food and drink to discover.

The Médoc

The Médoc is a tapering, triangular peninsula northwest of Bordeaux. The area is bordered by the Atlantic Ocean and the Gironde, whose influences combine to create a microclimate often ideal for vines. The name Médoc is derived from the Latin *in medio aquae*, 'in the midst of the waters'.

In the geographical centre of the peninsula at Saint-Seurin-de-Cadourne lies the border between the Haut-Médoc and Médoc. This also creates the division between these two wine appellations. The latter used to be called Bas-Médoc, but, as this had a somewhat negative ring, the 'Bas' has been dropped. If you look at the map you will see that Haut-Médoc lies in the south, nearer to Bordeaux. The two districts have equal vineyard areas – about 4,500 hectares each – but in terms of wine quality Haut-Médoc is rated rather higher.

Winegrowing in the Médoc did not begin until the 16th century, after prosperous merchants established wine estates of some importance there – earliest were in Macau and Margaux. From the 18th century it was increasingly ear-marked as a wine district, with signs of wealth appearing in the form of village churches and country houses. By the early 19th century most of the châteaux were beginning to be built. Today the area's economy depends on two important elements: winegrowing and tourism (the latter centred mainly on the Atlantic coast). The number of wine enthusiasts coming to the Médoc is growing considerably, with the result that more and more attention is being paid to facilities for recreation and château visits. In the summer many châteaux now open their *chais* and often put on exhibitions.

A visitor seeking evening entertainment should, look for it in Bordeaux not in the Médoc, however, for the peninsula is silent and deserted after sunset.

Left Château Beychevelle in St-Julien. This commune has the highest concentration of classed growths in the Médoc and its wines strike a balance between the structure and brilliance of Pauillac, to the north, and the refined, perfumed elegance of Margaux, further south.

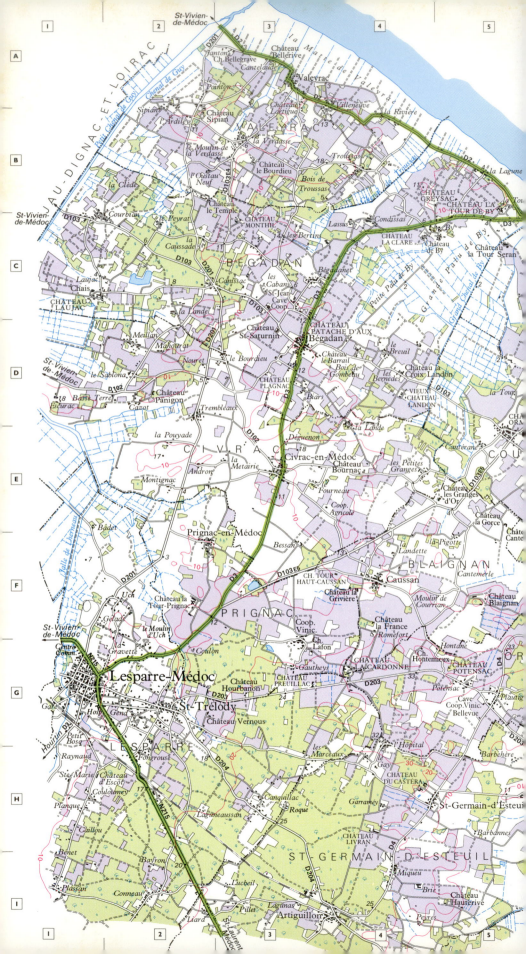

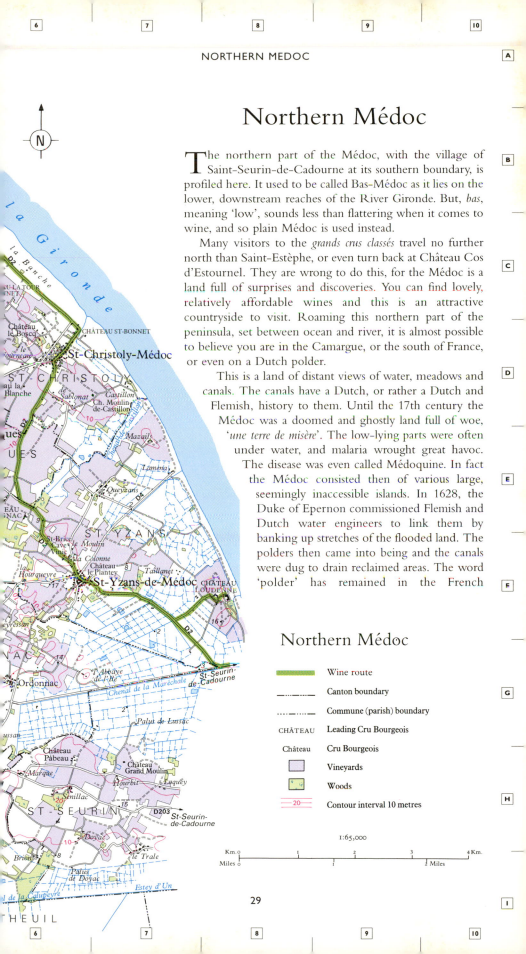

Northern Médoc

The northern part of the Médoc, with the village of Saint-Seurin-de-Cadourne at its southern boundary, is profiled here. It used to be called Bas-Médoc as it lies on the lower, downstream reaches of the River Gironde. But, *bas*, meaning 'low', sounds less than flattering when it comes to wine, and so plain Médoc is used instead.

Many visitors to the *grands crus classés* travel no further north than Saint-Estèphe, or even turn back at Château Cos d'Estournel. They are wrong to do this, for the Médoc is a land full of surprises and discoveries. You can find lovely, relatively affordable wines and this is an attractive countryside to visit. Roaming this northern part of the peninsula, set between ocean and river, it is almost possible to believe you are in the Camargue, or the south of France, or even on a Dutch polder.

This is a land of distant views of water, meadows and canals. The canals have a Dutch, or rather a Dutch and Flemish, history to them. Until the 17th century the Médoc was a doomed and ghostly land full of woe, '*une terre de misère*'. The low-lying parts were often under water, and malaria wrought great havoc. The disease was even called Médoquine. In fact the Médoc consisted then of various large, seemingly inaccessible islands. In 1628, the Duke of Epernon commissioned Flemish and Dutch water engineers to link them by banking up stretches of the flooded land. The polders then came into being and the canals were dug to drain reclaimed areas. The word 'polder' has remained in the French

Northern Médoc

▬▬▬	Wine route
–·–·–	Canton boundary
·····–··–	Commune (parish) boundary
CHÂTEAU	Leading Cru Bourgeois
Château	Cru Bourgeois
▨	Vineyards
▨	Woods
—20—	Contour interval 10 metres

1:65,000

Km.0   1   2   3   4 Km.
Miles 0   2 Miles

NORTHERN MEDOC

HOTELS

GAILLAN-EN-MEDOC
Château Layauga
T: 05 56 41 26 03, F: 05 56 41 19 52
Luxury hotel/restaurant, with seven
rooms at prices from around FF650.
Good cuisine with dishes of great
refinement. A great relief to find this
here in the Médoc. Set menus start
at around FF200. In autumn the *cèpes
au jus de truffes* are delightful. There
is an excellent wine list.

QUEYRAC
Hôtel des Vieux Acacias
T: 05 56 59 80 63, F: 05 56 59 85 93
Nice hotel in its own little park, for
which it has won awards. A breakfast
surprise here is the melon jam. Room
prices from about FF250.

RESTAURANTS

ST-CHRISTOLY
La Maison du Douanier
T: 05 56 41 35 25
Near the harbour, the terrace has
views over the river. Regional
specialities at affordable prices. Open
from mid-May to mid-September.

Main picture *Pastoral life on a
farm in St-Seurin in the Médoc.*
Above *Ducks and geese are farmed
for foie gras, which combines perfectly
with Sauternes.*
Far right *Château la Tour de By,
a cru bourgeois with an increasing
following for its quality and value.*

vocabulary since that time. The drained
marshes around Queyrac and Goulée
acquired the name Polder de Hollande,
and sometimes they were referred to as
La Petite Flandre du Médoc. An 18th-
century windmill near the village of
Vensac – still in use as a watermill – can
be visited on Sunday afternoons from
March to the end of September.

Not all the area is low-lying: there
are higher parts made up of gravel and
sand. These were eventually recognised
as especially suitable for winegrowing.
Excellent vineyards are often to be found on these gently
sloping *croupes*. Along the Atlantic shore are the dunes, vast
masses of sand which, with their great stretches of beach,
draw many tourists. This west coast of the Médoc is totally
different from the reclaimed land along the river. Here the
scene is one of mighty ocean breakers, great inland lakes
(such as Lac d'Hourtin), conifer forests and holiday resorts.

BLAIGNAN
Auberge des Vignobles
T: 05 56 09 04 81
Has a relaxed ambiance, with country cooking (*Côte de boeuf aux Cèpes*), affordable.

ST-GAUX
Le Relais chez Monique
T: 05 56 69 25 15
Simple *routiers* restaurant on the N215. Set lunchtime menu at around FF65, including wine.
Valeyrac/Port de Goulée La Guinguette
T: 05 56 41 37 48
A tremendously old-fashioned eating house by the harbour. A dozen oysters cost less than FF75.

RECOMMENDED PRODUCERS
BEGADAN
Château de By
Cru Bourgeois (By)
T: 05 56 41 51 53, F: 05 56 41 38 72
Deep-coloured wine of good quality, needing some time to develop.
Château La Clare
Cru Bourgeois (Condissas)
T: 05 56 41 50 61, F: 05 56 41 50 69
Intensely coloured, well-made Médoc with delicious red berry fruit on the finish.
Château Chantélys
Cru Bourgeois
T: 05 56 09 00 16, F: 05 56 58 17 20
A more than average Médoc, supple, fruity and slightly oaked.
Château Greysac
Cru Bourgeois
T: 05 56 73 26 56, F: 05 56 73 26 58
Smooth, harmonious wine, fairly complex.
Château Laujac
Cru Bourgeois
T: 05 56 41 50 12, F: 05 56 41 36 65
A dark, reserved, classic wine, rich in tannin and needing time to mature.

Up at the most northerly point of the Médoc you can look across to the mainland and the harbour and resort of Royan. In Le Verdon, a little village with a harbour near the Pointe de Grave, stands the Cordouan lighthouse, France's oldest. It even contains a royal chamber and a small chapel. Pointe de Grave is quite a popular spot for ornithologists as it is a good site to watch the northerly migration of birds in spring.

There are no vineyards near this northern tip. The Médoc's most northern vineyards are to be found a little way south in Jau-Dignac-et-Loirac, and Vensac. These are wine enclaves in the polders – a fact in itself to make them worth seeing. Between Dignac and Goulée you can turn onto the D102E, which runs in a straight line through the Polder de Hollande to Queyrac.

Château Patache d'Aux
Cru Bourgeois
T: 05 56 41 50 18, F: 05 56 41 54 65
The château is situated in the
centre of Bégadan on the spot where
stagecoaches used to stop. The wine
continues to improve but is already
a pleasant, full-bodied mouthful
when young.

Château Rollan de By
Cru Bougeois
T: 05 56 41 58 59, F: 05 56 41 37 82
Visits by appointment.

THE VINEYARDS

The grape varieties used in the Médoc AC are the same as in other districts of the peninsula. Permissable yields are a little higher than in Haut-Médoc, but many of the growers strive for better quality and often observe the most stringent standards. For those who are not averse to adventure in wine, and value personal contact with growers, the Médoc appellation is a good place to go. Visitors will generally be cordially received and wine prices are mostly reasonable.

As in the Haut-Médoc there are quite a few *crus bourgeois*, but there is also a large number of *crus artisans*. Although

Right and far right *Oysters are
a local delicacy. A large percentage
is farmed in the peaceful Bassin
d'Arcachon, an inlet of the
Atlantic Ocean, southwest of
the city of Bordeaux.*
Below *The impressive entrance
to Château La Tour de By. A well-
structured wine is produced here,
energetic in character, elegantly firm,
with fruit and oak nicely balanced.*

Château La Tour de By
Cru Bougeois
T: 05 56 41 50 03
There are two châteaux here. The
smaller, Château La Roque de By,
dates from the 18th century, the
larger from the 19th. Close to the
vineyard stands a former light tower –
worth climbing for the panoramic
view. Remarkably good wine with a
deep red colour and a stylish palate.

BLAIGNAN
Château Tour Haut-Caussan
T: 05 56 09 00 77, F: 05 56 09 06 24
Here one of the best Médocs is being
produced, from a vineyard around a
restored windmill.

ST-YZANS-DE-MEDOC
Château Loudenne
T: 05 56 73 17 80, F: 05 56 09 02 87
Elegant wines; warm, British-styled
hospitality. Lunches and tastings by
appointment.

back in the 19th century the *cru paysan* and *cru artisan* were
described in the standard work *Bordeaux et ses vins* (Cocks &
Ferret 1850 edition), the use of these terms on labels has
always been forbidden. This has now changed. A syndicate of
cru artisan growers has been set up, duly acknowledged by the
French agricultural ministry. It seems likely that the European
Community will sanction the term, too. In French the word
artisan means 'craftsman' and thus describes products made
in a non-industrial way. A craftsman-like wine will come
from a small estate, with 3 to 4 hectares of vineyard, and this
is generally the case with *crus artisans*. This, along with
certain quality requirements, is taken into account when the
wines are considered for *cru artisan* status. Many owners of a
cru artisan run their vineyards just as sidelines or hobbies.

THE WINE ROUTES

There are various routes for exploring the Médoc. A good
way is to begin on the D2 at Saint-Vivien-de-Médoc in the
north. The advantage of this road is that it will take you to
the little harbours of Goulée, By and Saint-Christoly. The
restaurant on the harbour at Goulée is a must. Other sites
worth seeing are the old lighthouse on the estate of
Château La Tour de By, and Bégadan with its historic
church containing an 11th-century apse.

At Château Loudenne, where you can have lunch if
you arrange it beforehand, there is a collection of
winegrowing equipment and tools. This estate
also makes a white wine. Lesparre, the 'capital' of
this part of the Médoc, is a small market town
with a congenial atmosphere. The square, 14th-
century tower here, l'Honneur de Lesparre, is
an historic monument. Information about the
area and its wines can be obtained from the
Maison du Médoc.

Then head across to Saint-Seurin-de-
Cadourne to begin exploring the Haut-Médoc.

Top *An elegant stairway leads up to Château la Lagune in Ludon.* Main picture *Fishing nets are a common sight on the Gironde.* Right *Château Bel-Air Lagrave, Moulis. This cru bourgeois produces charming wines with good fruitiness.*

CISSAC

HOTEL

Chateau Gugès
T: 05 56 59 58 04, F: 05 56 59 59 46
Seven rooms in a *maison bourgeoise*.
Country cooking. Affordable.

RECOMMENDED PRODUCERS

Château du Breuil
Cru Bourgeois
T: 05 56 59 58 13, F: 05 56 59 55 67
A beautiful estate where the château
dates from 13th century.

Château Cissac
Cru Bourgeois
T: 05 56 59 58 13, F: 05 56 59 55 67
An elegant, classy wine.

Château Hanteillan
Cru Bourgeois
T: 05 56 59 35 31, F: 05 56 59 31 51
Wine with feminine grace.

ST-SEURIN-DE-CADOURNE

RECOMMENDED PRODUCERS

**Châteaux Coufran and
Verdignan**
Crus Bourgeois
T: 05 56 59 31 02, F: 05 56 81 32 35
There is an unusually high proportion
of Merlot used for Château
Coufran. Verdignan is a stylish and
elegant wine.

Northern Haut-Médoc

Haut-Médoc is one of the two regional appellations of the peninsula (the other being Médoc, as we have seen). The Haut-Médoc begins at the northern boundary of the village of Saint-Seurin-de-Cadourne, and ends a few kilometres north of Bordeaux, near Château Magnol. The entire appellation covers about 4,200 vineyard hectares. Although its territory is interrupted here and there by smaller appellations, in this guide the north and south of the Haut-Médoc appellation are described separately, with the division made at Saint-Laurent.

Starting in the north of the territory (at Saint-Seurin-de-Cadourne) you can travel south back towards Bordeaux past some of the most fascinating wine sights of the entire region. First, you'll need to decide where to begin: either explore the 'Bas-Médoc' first (*see* pages 29–33), or head to Saint-Seurin and embark on the wine route from there.

To the west of Saint-Seurin-de-Cadourne, the three villages of Vertheuil, Cissac, and Saint-Sauveur form the border with the Médoc. As there are no *grands crus classés* châteaux here, people pay the area little attention. But, the countryside

of the northern Haut-Médoc is extremely attractive, with gently sloping hills and small, seemingly sleepy, picturesque villages – quite different from the rather flat terrain in the centre and south. At the wine estates here you will meet generally hospitable growers, pleased to invite you in and offer a glass of wine. The pleasure is doubled if you buy a couple of bottles. Places to eat, however, can be few and far between. There are village inns where a sandwich or a simple dish will be prepared, but they do little more than just satisfy hunger.

In general, connoisseurs rate wines from Saint-Seurin-de-Cadourne above those from Vertheuil, Saint-Sauveur and Cissac. Perhaps this is due to the soil and the situation, for Saint-Seurin is practically on the river. Geologically it is on an outlying section of the Saint-Estèphe plateau and a certain relationship in the wines cannot be denied. Château Sociando-Mallet is one of the typical estates.

Vertheuil, between Cissac and Pez, is another attractive place to head for. There are a couple of good châteaux and the little village itself has an improbably large church in 11th-century Romanesque and 15th-century styles, as well as a fine ancient churchyard. Also, there is an abbey that is listed as a protected monument. Exhibitions are held here.

Château Sociando-Mallet
Cru Bourgeois
T: 05 56 59 36 57, F: 05 56 59 70 88
Delicious blend of Cabernet and Merlot; a top *cru bourgeois*.

VERTHEUIL

RECOMMENDED PRODUCERS

Château le Bourdieu
Cru Bourgeois
T: 05 56 41 98 01, F: 05 56 41 99 32
Visits can include 17th-century abbey.
Château Le Meynieu
Cru Bourgeois
T: 05 56 41 98 17, F: 05 56 41 98 89
Spicy oak, berry fruit, tannins.

ST-SAUVEUR

RECOMMENDED PRODUCERS

Château Peyrabon
Cru Bourgeois
T: 05 56 59 57 10, F: 05 56 59 59 45
Well-made, good quality wine.
Château Ramage la Batisse
Cru Bourgeois
T: 05 56 59 57 24, F: 05 56 59 54 14
Balanced, deep and complex.

Saint-Estèphe

---·---·---	Canton boundary
---·---·---	Commune (parish) bound
CHÂTEAU	Cru Classé
Château	Cru Bourgeois
▮ (pink)	Premier Cru Classé vineya
▮ (purple)	Cru Classé vineyard
▯ (grey)	Other vineyard
▯ (green)	Woods
—20—	Contour interval 10 metre
▬ (green)	Wine route

*Left In addition to being famous
for its fine wines, St-Estèphe was
also a busy port, once vying in
importance with Bordeaux. All that
now remains is a tiny harbour used
mainly by fishing boats and yachts.*

SAINT-ESTEPHE

Travelling south from the tip of the Médoc, Saint-Estèphe is
the first of the major wine communes that you will reach.
Take the D204E3 east through the tiny village of Pez, and
you will find yourself there. You have now left behind the
fairly flat Médoc and entered a hillier, more romantic
area – a region of distant views.

At practically every crossroads and junction in
Saint-Estèphe there are signposts clearly showing
how to get to the châteaux. And these signs are
certainly needed, as all the small hills around
here mean you often cannot see sufficiently
far ahead and can easily lose your way.

Saint-Estèphe itself is a small village: the
core of the commune, surrounded by many
little hamlets. Cos (the 's' is pronounced) is
one example, a '*lieu-dit*'. In terms of its actual
vineyard area, Saint-Estèphe is the biggest of
the six community appellations in the Médoc. But
it has only five *grands crus classés* (not many compared
to the others). There are a good number of *crus bourgeois*,
however and, in recent years, Saint-Estèphe wines have
always been well placed in the competition for the
Coupe des Crus Bourgeois.

Saint-Estèphe forms the geographical centre of the
Médoc, equidistant from Pointe de Grave (57 kilometres

1:42,000

Km. 0 ———————— 1 ———————— 2 Km.
Miles 0 ———————————— 1 Mile

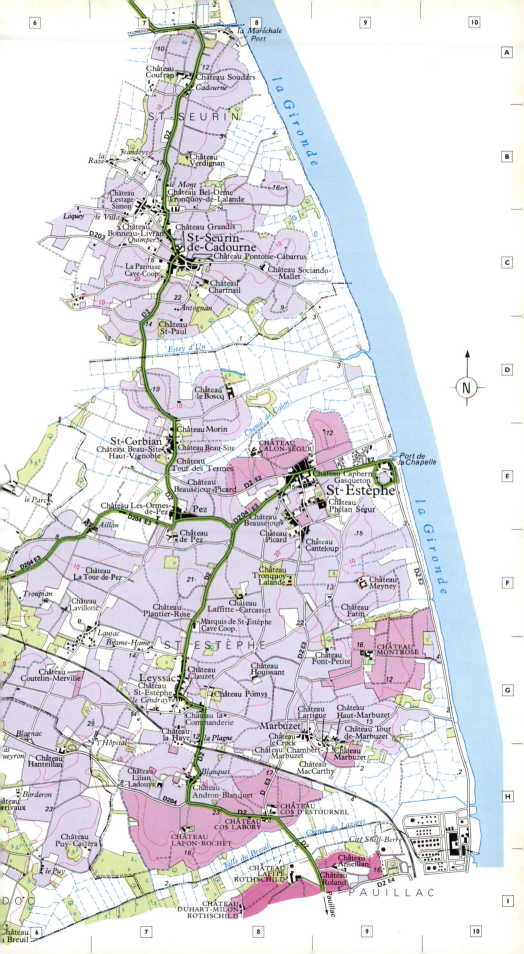

Far right *Château Marbuzet, a striking Louis XVI building with a small vineyard. It is also the second wine of Cos d'Estournel.*
Main picture *Château Lilian-Ladouys, the commune's rising star. Christian and Liliane Thiéblot established the 50-hectare property in 1989.*
Below *Fresh vegetables fill the market stalls throughout the region.*

away) and Bordeaux. The soil shows all the typical Médoc characteristics: layers of limestone, plenty of gravel, and sometimes clay; and the slopes here are ideal for vines in terms of natural drainage and distribution of water. The presence of the Gironde can be sensed, and is directly visible in many places. Château Montrose even used to have its own landing stage.

The village of Saint-Estephe has a fine church with a distinctive tower. According to local inhabitants, this (appropriately enough) was built to resemble a wine bottle. There are other vinicultural stopping points, too. Opposite the church is the Maison du Vin, where there is an impressive collection of wines, sold at the normal prices – the firmer Saint-Estèphe wines are eminently suitable for keeping. And from July 1st to September 15th, including weekends, the Marquis de Saint-Estèphe (the local cooperative) is open to visitors. It is a striking building standing beside the road and cannot be missed. If you want to eat, however, it is probably advisable to go on to Pauillac or Saint-Laurent.

SAINT-ESTEPHE

 HOTEL

Château Pomys
T: 05 56 59 32 26, F: 05 56 59 35 24
There are ten agreeable rooms here from around FF250.

SPECIAL INTEREST

A very pleasant route leads from Porte de la Chapelle, St-Estèphe's somewhat reduced harbour, to Pauillac. This little-known road is attractive as it is one of the few places where you can view and photograph the vineyards from the riverside.

RECOMMENDED PRODUCERS

Château Calon-Ségur
Grand Cru Classé (3ème)
T: 05 56 59 30 08, F: 05 56 59 71 51
In the 17th century this estate was the property of the rich and powerful Alexandre de Ségur, whose other possessions included Châteaux Lafite, Latour, Mouton and de Pez. Château Calon was, however, his favourite. Keep this wine for at least five years before drinking.

Château Cos d'Estournel
Grand Cru Classé (2ème)
T: 05 56 73 15 50, F: 05 56 59 72 59
One of the two stars of St-Estèphe. Intense, powerful, aromatic wine that keeps for many years. The d'Estournel family had various properties in

St-Estèphe in the 17th century, including a vineyard in the hamlet of Caux (the old spelling of Cos). 'Caux' proved in fact to be better than the other St-Estèphe vineyards, mainly because of the very gravelly slopes on which the vines were planted. Today Cos d'Estournel's modern winery and spacious cellar are perfectly maintained.

Château Le Crock
Cru Bourgeois
T: 05 56 86 49 25, F: 05 56 86 57 18
Wine that has attracted great interest in recent years – and deservedly so.

Château Haut-Marbuzet
Cru Bourgeois
T: 05 56 59 30 54, F: 05 56 59 70 87
Wine produced here usually is among the top ten of St-Estéphe. It has an expansive, sensual taste with a fair amount of oak (from new barrels).

Château Marbuzet
Cru Bourgeois
T: 05 56 73 15 50, F: 05 56 59 72 59
Worth viewing because of its architectural *grandeur*. The wine is attractive too.

Château Meyney
Cru Bourgeois
T: 05 56 59 30 31, F: 05 56 59 39 89
Classic and concentrated.

Château Montrose
Grand Cru Classé (2ème)
T: 05 56 59 30 12, F: 05 56 59 38 48
The second star in the St-Estèphe firmament. These wines are powerful, rich and harmonious. The estate is reminiscent of Alsace, keeping alive the memory of a former owner, Alsace-born Marthieu Dolfus, who acquired the château in 1866. There are still telling road signs on the estate – Rue d'Alsace, Rue de Mulhouse – although Montrose is now under the dynamic management of Jean-Louis Charmolüe.

Château les Ormes de Pez
Cru Bourgeois
T: 05 56 73 24 00, F: 05 56 59 26 42
Superior quality.

Château Phélan-Ségur
Cru Bourgeois
T: 05 56 59 30 09, F: 05 56 59 30 04
After heavy investment in the estate, the wines are, again, excellent.

Château Pomys
Cru Bourgeois
T: 05 56 59 32 26, F: 05 56 59 35 24
Substantial wines, but also supple, with a fine balance of oak and fruit.

ST-LAURENT MEDOC

HOTEL

La Renaissance
T & F: 05 56 59 40 29
Simple village inn with ten rooms.
A good place for a simple, tasty meal:
set menus from around FF100. Many
regional dishes, including *anguilles au
vert* (eels in wine and herb sauce).
The wine list is somewhat sparse.
Very simple rooms from about FF200.

RECOMMENDED PRODUCERS

Château Balac
Cru Bourgeois
T: 05 56 59 41 67, F: 05 56 59 93 90
Try the Cuvée Sélection Limitée.

Château Belgrave
Grand Cru Classé (5ème)
T & F: 05 56 59 40 20
Totally renovated in 1979, and the
quality of the wine is still improving.

Château Camensac
Grand Cru Classé (5ème)
T: 05 56 59 41 69, F: 05 56 59 41 73
Visits by appointment. Powerful wine.

Château Caronne Ste Gemme
Cru Bourgeois
T: 05 56 81 29 44, F: 05 56 51 71 51
Sound wine with good colour, style
and fruit character.

*Above The distinctive pagoda-like
architecture of Cos d'Estournel, one
of the commune's finest estates.
Main picture The Porte de la
Chapelle, the tiny harbour on the
Gironde at St-Estèphe. Until
1704, a much larger church
overlooked it, the Nôtre Dame
Entre-Deux-Arcs.*

SAINT-LAURENT-MEDOC

Saint-Laurent-Médoc is a true
winegrowing community for there are
no fewer than three *grands crus classés*
and some award-winning *crus bourgeois*
here. Yet it has no appellation of its own
(as neighbouring Listrac and Moulis
have) and growers are assigned to Haut-
Médoc. In 1982, however, a *syndicat
viticole* was set up, which is always the
first condition required by the INAO
(Institut National des Appellations
d'Origine) for a district ultimately to
acquire its own status.

Saint-Laurent is not on the D2 wine route but on the
N215 *voie rapide*: the quickest link between Bordeaux and
Pauillac. On an industrial estate beside the N215 is an
imposing, gleaming 'wine factory', where the world's best-
known brand wine, Mouton Cadet, is made and bottled.

Saint-Laurent's three *grands crus classés*, Châteaux Belgrave,
Camensac and La Tour Carnet, are situated on a sloping
plateau that stretches towards Saint-Julien. Their wines
therefore have much in common with those of Saint-Julien,
so much so that it might almost have been more logical to
admit Saint-Laurent Médoc into the Saint-Julien appellation.

Château Larose-Trintaudon
Cru Bourgeois
T: 05 56 59 41 72, F: 05 56 59 93 22
This is the Médoc's largest wine
estate: it belongs to the French
insurance company AGF and makes
reliable wine.

Château La Tour Carnet
Grand Cru Classé (4ème)
T: 05 56 73 30 90, F: 05 56 59 48 54
A fourth-growth *grand cru classé*
producing charming, elegant wines to
be drunk reasonably early.

The Saint-Laurent plateau is fairly high and very susceptible
to night frosts. In April 1991, for example, this led to a
disaster in which 80 per cent of the vines was affected by frost
in a single night. At its western edge it is well-wooded and,
with the one exception of Château de Cartujac, has no
winegrowing. These woods are cherished as places to look
for the famous *cèpes*, the *boletuses* (wild mushrooms) that taste
so marvellous as a garnish for red meat. Saint-Laurent-
Médoc itself has become a peaceful place since its bypass was
built, and there is hardly any traffic in the centre of the
village. It has an interesting church. A point worth noting in
Saint-Laurent is that one of the smallest Médoc wine estates,
Château le Bouscat, is situated here as well as Château
Larose-Trintaudon, the biggest of them all.

If you are travelling from Bordeaux and want to travel in
the opposite direction, from Saint-Laurent to Saint-Estèphe,
this is the route you should follow: first take the D206 and
then bear left just before Pauillac, towards Saint-Estèphe. At
the railway crossing in Pauillac you will get back on to the
D2 again. Shortly after passing Château Lafite-Rothschild
you cross the little Jalle de Breuil stream and, almost without
noticing, you come to the Pauillac boundary. You then
climb to the remarkable Cos d'Estournel with its pagoda
towers. Bear right here and head past Lalande into Saint-
Estèphe itself.

Above *One of many ornate
sculptures found on the estates
throughout Bordeaux. This one
stands in the grounds of Château
Montrose in St-Estèphe.*

PAUILLAC

The Médoc has no capital in any legal sense, but many connoisseurs are of the opinion that, if there were to be one, the small town of Pauillac (population just under 6,000) would well merit this title. The big difference between the Pauillac appellation and the other wine communities is that its château names are more important than that of the commune itself. Professor Emile Peynaud once expressed it thus: 'Here the château provides the name and the fame'. There are 18 *grand cru* châteaux in total, and of the Médoc's four *premiers grands crus,* three are from Pauillac. Even the cooperative has a more than merely good reputation, though its members are declining in number as the region's reputation enables each château to make and market its own wines.

This little harbour town which sits on the River Gironde differs also in its history. Many surveys of the wine districts of the Médoc began with the arrival of the Romans, but this was not the case for Pauillac. Until the 14th century, the Bordeaux vineyards certainly extended no further north than Macau, reaching the Margaux area in the 15th century. It was only in the course of the 17th century that vineyard plantations spread any further north in the Médoc region. And winegrowing did not develop fully in the Pauillac area until later on in the 18th century, when the Bordeaux merchants first began to invest in it.

For hundreds of years, however, the town of Pauillac had benefited from its favourable situation on the

Pauillac

――·――·―	Canton boundary
――···――···―	Commune (parish) boundary
CHÂTEAU	Cru Classé
Château	Cru Bourgeois
▨	Premier Cru Classé vineyard
▨	Cru Classé vineyard
▢	Other vineyard
▨	Woods
═20═	Contour interval 10 metres
▬	Wine route

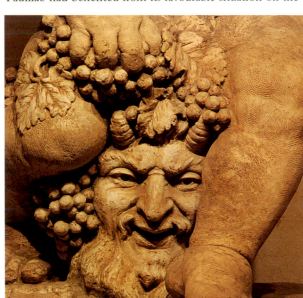

Left *The importance of wine to the Médoc, both culturally and economically, is reflected in sculptures and architecture.*

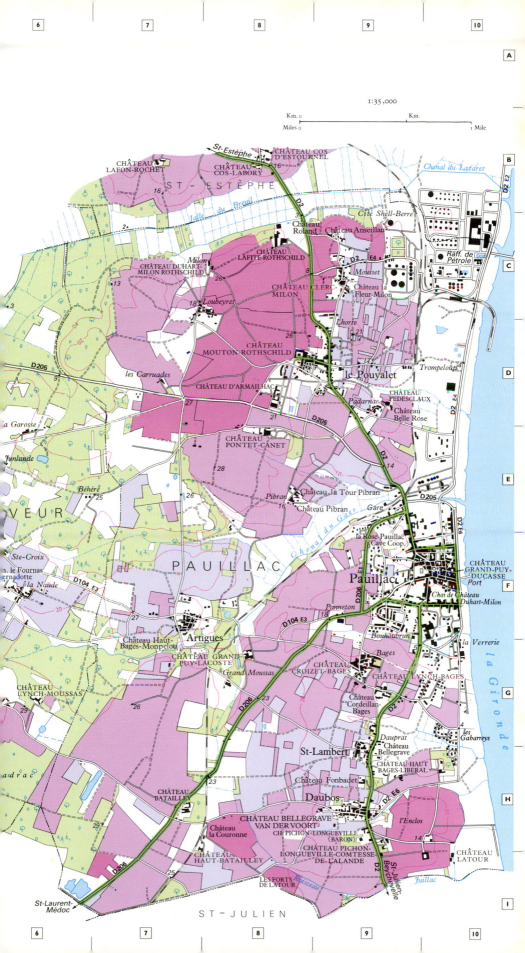

Above and right *Pauillac, the 'capital' of the Médoc, is a good place to stop off for shopping or simply to take a break from visiting châteaux.* Far right *Unlike the other major wine towns in the Médoc, Pauillac is situated directly on the Gironde.*

PAUILLAC

HOTELS

Château Cordeillan-Bages
T: 05 56 59 24 24, F: 05 56 59 01 89
Excellent hotel/restaurant, a member of Relais & Châteaux. The rooms are luxurious, at prices from about FF1,000. Lounge and restaurant are most tastefully furnished. The quality of the cuisine is usually very good, with a distinct classic basis. The wine list is simply splendid, with all the famous Médoc names. Set menus start below FF200. Recommended: the lunch menu from around FF350, including wine and coffee.

Hôtel de France et Angleterre
T: 05 56 59 01 20, F: 05 56 59 02 31
This quayside hotel/restaurant has been rebuilt and refurbished. Attractive rooms with modern furnishings, named after different châteaux: always ask for one at the back. Menus, from around FF100, of decent country cooking. Large wine list. All in all, a pleasant and affordable place to stay in the heart of the Médoc.

Gironde. The surrounding infrastructure was good and the larger sailing ships were able to take on full cargoes here. An added benefit of the port was the fact that it was a convenient sailing distance, of one tide, from both the Atlantic in one direction and the city of Bordeaux in the other. Because of this Pauillac was granted maritime rights in the Middle Ages, so foreign ships were obliged to take on board a pilot and four seamen from the town. Seafarers awaiting the turn of the tide stayed in Pauillac, and many a tavern undoubtedly did well out of this. Its docks were also used many times by boats sailing towards England to strengthen relationships between the two countries. In the 1700s, the influential businessman Lafayette was particularly active in this respect.

Today the yacht harbour is well-known for its excellent facilities. The Maison du Vin stands right beside it, where the quay starts. Wines from many Pauillac châteaux can be

RESTAURANT

La Salamandre
T: 05 56 59 08 68
Simple place to eat on the quay, better known locally as 'Chez Johan'. Always busy at lunchtimes. Low-priced set menus, fish and other seafood dishes. Not bad; nothing out of the ordinary.

SPECIAL INTEREST

The annual Médoc marathon has a wine connection: the whole of this unique 42-kilometre course runs through the vineyards, starting and finishing in Pauillac. A carnival mood prevails, giving the race a very special atmosphere. Held mid-September.

RECOMMENDED PRODUCERS

Château d'Armailhac
Grand Cru Classé (5ème)
T: 05 56 59 22 22, F: 05 56 73 20 44
The former Mouton-d'Armailhacq was bought in 1933 by Baron Philippe de Rothschild of Mouton Rothschild, the adjoining estate. From 1956– 1974 the estate was called Mouton Baron Philippe; 'Baron' changed to 'Baronne' in 1975 in honour of the Baron's late wife, Pauline. In 1989, it reverted back to the original: d'Armailhac. Alluringly aromatic, with lovely fruit.

Château Batailley
Grand Cru Classé (5ème)
T: 05 56 00 00 70, F: 05 56 52 29 54
Visit this estate to see the park: the trees come from all over the world. Decent wine, with soft tannin, and a pleasant, fruity character.

Château Fonbadet
Cru Bourgeois
T: 05 56 59 02 11, F: 05 56 59 27 37
Deeply-coloured, classic Pauillac.

Château Grand-Puy Ducasse
Grand Cru Classé (5ème)
T: 05 56 01 30 10, F: 05 56 79 23 57
Meaty, juicy, with lovely aromas of fruit and a fine touch of wood.

Château Grand-Puy Lacoste
Grand Cru Classé (5ème)
T: 05 56 59 06 66, F: 05 56 59 27 37
Powerful, elegant, complex wine. There is a canal-side garden nearby.

Château Lafite-Rothschild
Grand Cru Classé (1er)
T: 05 56 73 18 18, F: 56 59 26 83
Baron Eric de Rothschild took over in 1980. Refined, subtly complex in aroma, palate and finish – one of the world's most stunning wines. The 18th-century château can't be visited but the splendid new cellars can.

bought here at current prices, and you can obtain information about visits, and guided tours around them. Roughly in the middle of the waterfront boulevard stands the Château Grand Puy-Ducasse with its *chai* and *cuverie*. Its vineyards actually lie outside the town, and were originally pieced together from a number of different parcels of land during the 1740s.

The highly esteemed Château Mouton Rothschild has a unique and splendid wine museum set up by the late Baron Philippe de Rothschild and his wife. A visit here is an absolute must for any wine-lover. Visits and guided tours can be arranged by appointment only (*telephone: 05 56 59 22 22*). Take care to visit on the right day as the museum is closed at weekends, on public holidays, and throughout August.

Pauillac's winegrowing region consists of two parts: the little Chenal du Gaer stream, which flows into the Gironde behind the station, can be taken as the dividing line. This natural boundary results from the presence of two practically identical gravel plateaux. On the northern one sit the châteaux of Lafite-Rothschild, Mouton Rothschild and Pontet-Canet. Among the châteaux to the south, towards Saint-Julien, are Château Latour, Château Lynch–Bages and

Above *Work taking place amongst the vines at Château Pontet-Canet, neighbour of Château Mouton Rothschild in Pauillac.*
Right *Pauillac is famous for its milk-fed lamb, agneau de lait, which is wonderful served with the local wines.*
Far right *The splendid Château Mouton Rothschild.*

Château Latour
Grand Cru Classé (1er)
T: 05 56 73 19 80, F: 05 56 73 19 81
Derives its name from a former fortress on the site: the solitary domed tower in the grounds today is not the remains of a medieval fortification but a *pigeonnier.* A wine of superlatives: strong, intense and reliable – has been trumping its rivals for decades. Long bottle-ageing is essential.

Château Lynch-Bages
Grand Cru Classé (5ème)
T: 05 56 73 24 00, F: 05 56 59 26 42
Great, classic Pauillac: red berry fruits dominate a harmonious palate. It far exceeds its *5ème cru* classification.

Château Mouton Rothschild
Grand Cru Classé (1er in 1973)
T: 56 59 22 22, F: 05 56 73 20 44
No other Bordeaux estate has had so much published about it, and no other *propriétaire* has been so much written about as the late Baron Philippe. When the management of Mouton passed to him in 1922 it was more of a farm than a château. With great vision and tenacity, the Baron successfully made Mouton one of the most respected and visited wine estates in the world; and this despite the fact he was poet, playwright, film and theatre director and racing driver. With his American wife, Pauline, he created a unique wine museum, and since 1946

the two Pichons. Château Latour is in the separate hamlet of Saint-Lambert, which used to be a part of the Saint-Julien commune.

Nowadays there is also white wine made in Pauillac. Lynch-Bages released one, Lynch Blanc, at the end of 1991. And at the beginning of 1993, Château Mouton Rothschild brought out a white estate wine called Aile d'Argent. These are not allowed full AC Pauillac status, and must be sold under the Bordeaux appellation, but there is talk of a Médoc Blanc category for the future. Up until 1956 many châteaux produced white wine, but mostly for their own consumption. In February 1956, however, a hard frost destroyed a great many of the region's vines. In the subsequent replanting, white grape varieties were not even considered.

Today there is also great interest in the so-called 'second wines' of the *grands crus classés*. This must surely be the result of the higher demands being placed on the top estates. More stringent selection of the grapes at harvest means a higher proportion of the fruit is found not to be good enough for the *grand cru* itself – with the result that wine at the next level down benefits, gaining in power and style. Les Forts de Latour is often quoted as the most celebrated of these second wines. Strictly speaking, however, it is no longer a second wine but altogether a *cru* in its own right. Another

commissioned a work by a famous artist each year for the Mouton label. The Baron's greatest coup was the promotion of Mouton Rothschild in 1973 from first of the second-growths to its rightful place as a *premier cru* – the only change ever made to the 1855 classification. It is formidable, with a sumptuous cedarwood and red fruits and berries aroma.

Château Pibran
Cru Bourgeois
T: 05 56 73 24 20, F: 05 56 73 17 28
Racy and intense, with plenty of colour and tannin. A better *cru bourgeois*.

Château Pichon-Longueville
Grand Cru Classé (2ème)
T: 05 56 73 24 20, F 05 56 73 17 28
Turrets and steep-pitched roofs characterise this château. In 1990 it was completely renovated under the auspices of Jean-Michel Cazes and AXA-Millésimes. The new cellars are of striking design and the wine is better than ever: ripe fruit and oak ensure a firm yet smooth, elegant mouthful.

Château Pichon-Longueville Comtesse de Lalande
Grand Cru Classé (2ème)
T: 05 56 59 19 40, F: 05 56 59 26 56
A wine of impressive quality: rich in wood and fruit and always perfectly balanced. The Comtesse is the larger portion of what was once a single estate; the balance is Baron.

Château Pontet-Canet
Grand Cru Classé (5ème)
T: 05 56 59 04 04, F: 05 56 59 26 63
The winery is enormous. The loft over the *cuvier* can seat up to 600 (for receptions) and the high-ceilinged cask cellar is quite cathedral-like. The wine is dark and concentrated with lots of fruit and a long finish.

renowned Pauillac second wine is the Carruades (formerly called Moulins de Carruades) from Lafite-Rothschild. Château Mouton Rothschild has Le Petit Mouton de Mouton Rothschild as its second wine.

Pauillac's well-known cooperative has the harmonious name of La Rose Pauillac. It markets a Pauillac appellation wine under the same name. Visitors are welcome there six days of the week. You will find the cooperative near the railway station in the Rue du Maréchal Joffre.

And no wine-lover leaving Pauillac for Saint-Julien could ever simply drive past the new buildings at Château Pichon-Longueville Baron: in fact you pass between the *chais* on the D2. The château itself, which certainly deserves a visit, is 19th-century in style, but beside it are very modern winery and cellar structures, designed with great artistry. Pichon-Longueville Baron is a futuristic monument based on the 21st-century wine-drinker. Visitors are welcome on any day.

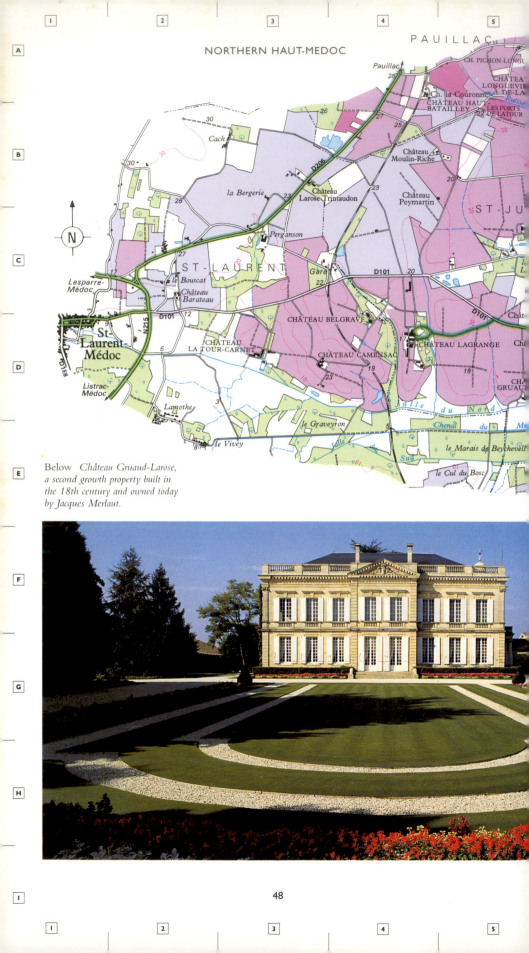

Below *Château Gruaud-Larose,*
a second growth property built in
the 18th century and owned today
by Jacques Merlaut.

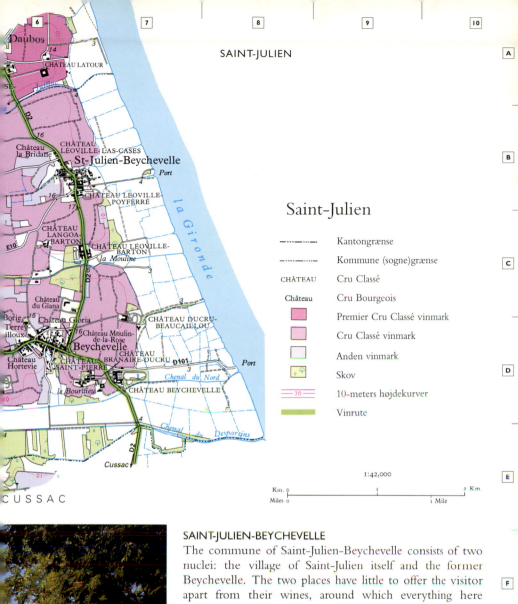

Saint-Julien

—···—···—	Kantongrænse
—·······—	Kommune (sogne)grænse
CHÂTEAU	Cru Classé
Château	Cru Bourgeois
🟪	Premier Cru Classé vinmark
🟪	Cru Classé vinmark
⬜	Anden vinmark
🟨	Skov
~20~	10-meters højdekurver
▬▬	Vinrute

1:42,000

Km. 0   1   2 Km.
Miles 0   1 Mile

SAINT-JULIEN-BEYCHEVELLE

The commune of Saint-Julien-Beychevelle consists of two nuclei: the village of Saint-Julien itself and the former Beychevelle. The two places have little to offer the visitor apart from their wines, around which everything here seems to revolve. Of the very greatest importance are the 11 *grands crus classés* châteaux. Producing these wines takes up 85 per cent of the vineyard area – covering some 910 hectares. But there are quite a few other interesting châteaux to explore.

Approaching on the D2 from Pauillac, you will first reach Saint-Julien itself, with an interesting church as one of its key sights to see. The village is enclosed by the châteaux of the three Léovilles. The Marquis de Léoville's estate was originally one of the biggest in the Médoc until, after the Revolution, it was split into three: Léoville-las-Cases (the largest), Léoville-Poyferré and Léoville-Barton (the smallest). Although the other two Léovilles are of a high calibre, Léoville-las-Cases has had the most publicity in the last ten years. This is not surprising, for the owner's aim has been to compete with the *premiers grands crus classés*. He as been successful every year, with unfortunate consequences for the price of his wine. Less affluent

ST-JULIEN-BEYCHEVELLE

RECOMMENDED PRODUCERS

Château Beychevelle
Grand Cru Classé (4ème)
T: 05 56 73 20 70
This 17th-century château is one of the most beautiful in the Médoc. The wine is intense and calls for patience – the rewards are worth the wait.

Below The fourth-growth Château Saint-Pierre.

Château Branaire
Grand Cru Classé (4ème)
T: 05 56 59 25 86, F: 05 56 59 16 26
Fine flowery aromas and elegant finish.
Château Ducru-Beaucaillou
Grand Cru Classé (2ème)
T: 05 56 59 05 20, F 05 56 59 27 37
Set majestically against the east (riverside) slope of the more southerly of the St-Julien gravel plateaus. The façade, flanked by two stout Victorian towers, looks towards the Gironde, and a magnificent park enhances the view. The wine is complex, and perfectly balanced.
Château Gloria
T: 05 56 59 08 18, F 05 56 59 16 18
Balanced, generous wine.
Château Gruaud-Larose
Grand Cru Classé (2ème)
T: 05 56 73 15 20, F: 05 56 59 64 72
One of the most finely tuned wines from this village. The large château with its Louis XVI salons and beautiful park was totally renovated in 1995.

enthusiasts find his second wine, the Clos du Marquis, more accessible. In recent years Léoville-las-Cases has certainly reached the *grand cru classé* level.

The name of Henri Martin is indissolubly linked with Saint-Julien. He was not only its *maire* and a grower, but also one of the founders of the wine fraternity *Commanderie du Bontemps de Médoc et des Graves*. Martin, who owned Château Saint-Pierre, died in 1991 and is commemorated by a bronze bust, which stands in a little garden at Beychevelle, in a sharp bend in the D2 beside the chateaux. Just before this bend you will see a huge wine bottle – a not very subtle form of publicity that Saint-Julien nowadays does not need. An interesting but little-known detail here is that the three châteaux of Beychevelle, Branaire, and Gruaud-Larose were built in the 18th century in line with one another. Château Beychevelle is the most famous, especially for its imposing frontage, and visitors should also take care to look round the back where there is a superb view of the River Gironde.

Château Lagrange
Grand Cru Classé (3ème)
T: 05 56 59 23 63, F: 05 56 59 26 09
This is one of the most interesting
Médoc châteaux to visit. Since it was
taken over by the Japanese drinks
giant Suntory towards the end of
1983, almost everything on this big
estate has been altered or renovated.
The wine – a classic, delicious
St-Julien – is still improving.

Château Langoa-Barton
Grand Cru Classé (3ème)
T: 05 56 59 06 05, F: 05 56 59 14 29
One of the gems of the Médoc: a
chartreuse built above cellars, with a
lovely terraced garden behind. The
only *grand cru* still owned and
inhabited by the same family as in
1855. The wine itself is very like its
big brother, Léoville-Barton, but with
rather less depth.

Château Léoville-Barton
Grand Cru Classé (2ème)
(For details see Langoa above)
The smallest Léoville, owned by
the Barton family, who came from
Ireland early in the 18th century.
Deep-coloured, rich and powerfully
structured wine.

Château Léoville-las-Cases
Grand Cru Classé (2ème)
T: 05 56 59 25 26, F: 05 56 59 18 33
After the French Revolution, the
estate of the Marquis de Léoville was

Above *Barrels stacked in
the cellar of the 17th-century
Château Beychevelle.*
Main picture *This aerial view
of Gruaud-Larose demonstrates
how dramatically the châteaux
of the Médoc stand out against
the flat, often dull landscape.*

split into three: the present châteaux Léoville-las-Cases (the largest), Léoville-Poyferré and Léoville-Barton. Perfectionist Michel Delon produces a memorable wine, rather tough when young, but developing aristocratic quality with time.

Château Léoville-Poyferré
Grand Cru Classé (2ème)
T: 05 56 59 08 30, F: 05 56 59 60 09
Still a little undervalued, but deserves its second growth status for its pure breeding, fruit, and length of aftertaste.

Château Moulin de la Rose
Cru Bourgeois
T: 05 56 59 08 45, F: 05 56 59 73 94
Excellent wine, rich in colour.

Château St-Pierre
Grand Cru Classé (4ème)
T: 05 56 59 08 18, F: 05 56 59 16 18
Rounded, approachable wine. Quality is still improving.

Beychevelle formerly belonged to the dukes of Epernon. One of them was an Admiral of France and the story goes that seamen coming up the River Gironde had to show due respect to the admiral by lowering the sails of their boats when they came in sight of his château. In the Gascon vernacular the expression was *bacha velo*, in other words, *baisser la voile* or 'lower the sails' and from this Beychevelle is reputed to derive its name. Evidently they still appreciate such courtesies in Saint-Julien, for the visitor crossing the commune boundary will read a sign saying '*passants, vous entrez dans le très célèbre et très illustré cru de Saint-Julien. Saluez*'.

At Château Branaire an impressive *chai* has been built with a laboratory-like tasting area in its centre. And between châteaux Beychevelle and Saint-Laurent lies the large estate of Château Lagrange which, since 1983, has belonged to the Japanese drinks giant, Suntory. Practically everything on this estate, from the buildings to the vineyards, has been rebuilt, renewed, revitalised or refurbished, and it is now one of the finest properties in the Médoc – and one that's well worth the visit if you have time. With all the subsidiary buildings nearby, the château rather resembles a small 19th-century village.

Above *Léoville-Poyferré, one of the three Léovilles comprising the Marquis de Léoville's estate which was broken up in 1789.*
Right *Château Beychevelle. Built in the 17th century, the château is regarded as one of the most beautiful in the Médoc.*
Far right *Traditional gates hide high technology at Château Lagune, owned by Champagne Ayala.*

Château Talbot
Grand Cru Classé (4ème)
T: 05 56 73 21 50, F: 05 56 73 21 51
With more than 100ha of vines, this is the largest property in St-Julien. It is named after John Talbot, Earl of Shrewsbury, who lodged here in 1453 before dying in battle with the French at Castillon. Attractive, noble wine with charm and good structure.

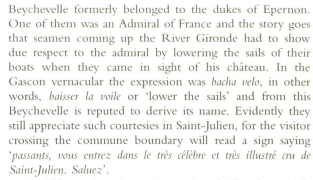

Southern Haut-Médoc

CUSSAC-FORT-MEDOC

There are two hamlets with 'Cussac' in their names, Vieux Cussac and Cussac-Fort-Médoc, but it is the latter that is mostly used for this commune.

Before you actually reach Cussac (near the D2 between Cussac and Saint-Julien) you will see Château Lanessan, which well deserves to have *grand cru* status. Besides its wine, it is renowned for its carriage museum, the Musée du Cheval, which is definitely worth a visit. It has a well-maintained collection of 19th- and early 20th-century carriages, accommodated in the splendid former stables. Also worthy of note is Château Beaumont, which for some years has been the property of a French pension fund. It has restored the building to its full former splendour, and the vineyards have been largely replanted.

Cussac really does have a fort, by the river. It was the creation of the military architect Vauban, who also converted the citadel at Blaye into an ingenious defensive work. The purpose of these forts was the protection of Bordeaux – mainly against English men-of-war. The Cussac fort spent years in great neglect, but is now slowly being restored to its earlier glory. Jazz concerts (amongst other events) are held here in summer and provide an excellent opportunity for visitors to take in the surroundings. To reach Fort-Médoc you turn on to the D2/E9 in Vieux Cussac.

The Cussac-Fort-Médoc cooperative bears the aristocratic name of Les Chevaliers du Roi Soleil, 'Knights of the Sun King'. This is the Médoc's smallest cooperative with around 20 members, and it has a reputation for producing decent wines.

Central Médoc

----------	Kantongrænse
-----------	Kommune (sogne) grænse
CHÂTEAU	Cru Classé
Château	Cru Bourgeois
▮	Cru Classé vinmark
▯	Anden vinmark
▮	Skov
— 50 —	10-meters højdekurver
▬▬▬	Vinrute

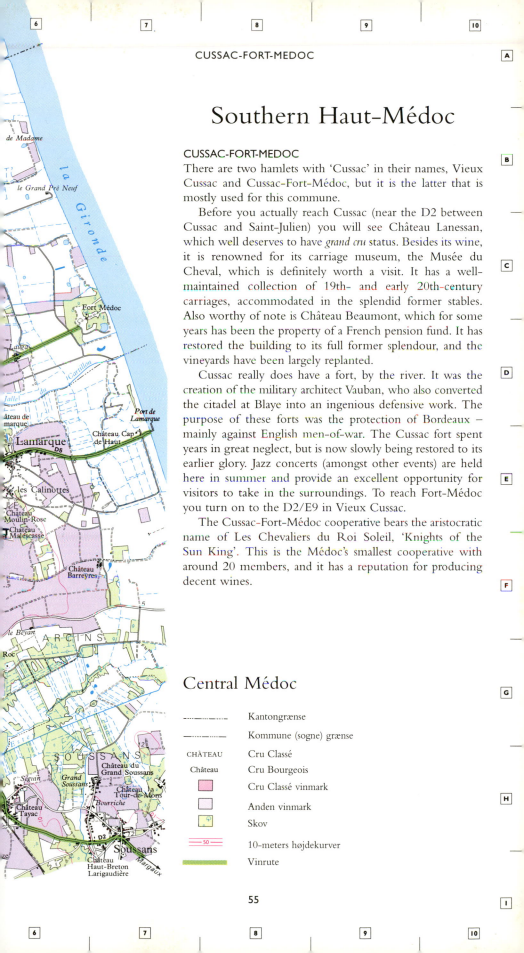

Right and below right *Images from around the historical town of Lamarque: an old inscription on a wall and the Château de Lamarque, a preserved medieval fortress.*

CUSSAC-FORT-MÉDOC

RECOMMENDED PRODUCERS

Château Beaumont
Cru Bourgeois
T: 05 56 58 92 29, F: 05 56 58 90 94
Elegant wine with a lingering hint of blackcurrants and oak. Much new planting should give more depth.

Château Lanessan
Cru Bourgeois Supérieur
T: 56 58 94 80
One of the very best Haut-Médocs, intense in taste, rich in tannin and with great potential for ageing. Also has a carriage museum.

Château du Moulin Rouge
Cru Bourgeois
T: 05 56 58 91 13, F: 05 56 58 93 68
Big, powerful wines.

Château Tour du Haut Moulin
Cru Bourgeois
T: 05 56 58 91 10, F: 05 56 58 99 30
A great wine with a rich, powerful length and supple tannins. Visitors are welcomed in the small château; the cellars are situated on the road to the fort.

LAMARQUE

RESTAURANTS

Relais du Médoc
T: 05 56 58 92 27
Friendly local restaurant with good, appetising food. Classic regional dishes. Set menus from about FF100, and a more expensive *menu Médocain* (including wine). There are a few simple rooms here at less than FF200.

L'Escale
T: 05 56 58 92 21
Next to the spot where the ferry leaves for Blaye. Simple, inexpensive. Emphasis on *fruits de mer*. Also has a bar.

RECOMMENDED PRODUCERS

Château du Cartillon
Cru Bourgeois
T: 05 57 43 01 44, F: 05 57 43 08 75
Renovated château. Classic wine.

Château de Lamarque
Cru Bourgeois
T: 05 56 58 90 03, F: 05 56 58 93 43
Beautiful castle, immaculately maintained. The wines are nice too: strikingly smooth, often velvety Haut-Médoc with a firm core.

LAMARQUE

The little village of Lamarque owes its reputation to water and to wine. Its connection with water is the ferry that links it with Blaye on the opposite bank of the Gironde. The wine element is given impressive form in Château de Lamarque.

The château was originally built as a fortress against attacks from the Gironde; you can reach it by way of a tree-lined drive. Parts of it are 11th- and 12th-century (the cellars and chapel), but the main structure dates from around the 14th. Inside there is a great hall with portrait paintings and fabulous antique furniture. The inner courtyard is also beautiful. Both the Duke of Gloucester and the French King Henry IV have lived there and today it is the heart of a top wine estate.

From the little harbour at Lamarque there is a fine view across the water to the right bank of the Gironde.

On the way to Arcins you pass Château Maucaillou, with an interesting museum: the Musée des Arts et Métiers de la Vigne et du Vin. All stages of growing and making wine are displayed, together with a most ingenious 'scent organ', with which you can smell the different fragrances of wine.

ARCINS

However minuscule this village may be, there are good reasons for stopping here, namely the châteaux and a charming restaurant. Arcins is situated just outside the Margaux appellation on the D2. The wines are given the Haut-Médoc appellation, but they are very like those of Margaux.

The region has a turbulent history. Although Château d'Arcins, for example, was producing 140,000 litres of wine a year in 1850, the arrival of phylloxera wrought such havoc that this scale of production fell drastically. Many wine estates fell into decay. Even as recently as a generation ago there were hardly any vineyards remaining at all. Increasing prosperity fortunately brought a turnaround, and investing in this former 'no man's land' became fashionable again. Châteaux Arnauld and d'Arcins represent this well, having been totally renewed and updated. Both are open to visitors.

MOULIS

To get to Moulis you turn right in Arcins where the sign points to Château Chasse-Spleen. This route takes you to the famous Poujeaux plateau. If you turn left south of Grand Poujeaux the road brings you to the village of Moulis.

This is the smallest village appellation. Winegrowing began here in the Middle Ages on a purely ecclesiastical basis. Moulis was the second religious centre of the region after Bordeaux, with four priories and 34 parishes, and was therefore an important supplier of communion wine. In fact the Moulis legend tells of how a pope commissioned the building of two identical churches, one in Rome and the other in Moulis. The church completed first would become the centre of the whole Catholic faith. Moulis did not stand a chance. In a more concrete form there remains a beautiful Romanesque church here with fine statuary and carving, within and without.

Both 'Moulis' and 'Moulis-en-Médoc' are used as wine appellations, but Moulis is more usual. Moulis' total vineyard area is 600 hectares, with the gravel of the Poujeaux plateau in the east, clay soils with lime in the northwest.

There are no grands crus classés in Moulis, but over the years some of its wines – notably

Château Malescasse
Cru Bourgeois
T: 05 56 58 90 09, F: 05 56 58 97 89
Worth visiting.

ARCINS

RESTAURANTS

Le Lion d'Or
T: 05 56 58 96 79
One of the best places to eat in the whole Médoc, with an international reputation. Besides the main menu, owner and chef Barrier still keeps the simple lunchtime *menu familiale* at something below FF100. *Plats du jour* are written on a board beside the road outside. Good wines.

RECOMMENDED PRODUCERS

Château d'Arcins
Cru Bourgeois
T: 05 56 58 91 29, F: 05 57 88 50 26
From 10 to 96 hectares in 20 years.
Château Arnauld
Cru Bourgeois
T: 05 57 88 50 34, F: 05 57 88 50 35
An elegant, lively wine.

MOULIS

HOTELS

CASTELNAU-DE-MEDOC
Restaurant-hôtel Les Landes
T: 05 56 58 73 80, F: 05 56 88 81 59
Simple village hotel; cooking is good and this is where wine-buyers quite often stay. Rooms from a little under FF200. Set menus start around FF100.
Château Biston
T: 05 56 58 22 13
Good *chambres d'hôte*. Open March to November; costs around FF300.

RECOMMENDED PRODUCERS

Château Biston-Brillette
Cru Bourgeois
T: 05 56 58 22 86, F: 05 56 58 13 16
Aromatic, meaty wine that can be
drunk early, but has enough tannin
to be kept.

Château Chasse-Spleen
Cru Bourgeois
T: 05 56 58 02 37, F: 05 56 58 05 70
Exceptionally reliable wine, even in
lesser years. Firm in taste with hints
of fruit and oak on the nose. Not
filtered. A masterly Moulis.

Château Maucaillou
Cru Bourgeois
T: 05 56 58 01 23, F: 05 56 58 00 88
A wine with supple, sinewy strength
and grace. Deep colour, elegant
bouquet and a refined palate with firm
tannin. The château has a splendid
wine museum across the street.

Château Moulin-à-Vent
Cru Bourgeois
T: 05 56 58 15 79, F: 05 56 58 12 05
Meatiness, ripe fruit and tannin in a
pleasing, rounded mouthful. A reliable
Moulis estate. Situated next to the
N215, it has an impressive cellar that
holds 1,200 barrels.

Château Poujeaux
Cru Bourgeois
T: 05 56 58 02 96, F: 05 56 58 01 25
Classic, mouth-filling Médoc that can
be unforthcoming at first. Alongside
the tannin there is also elegance and
good fruit.

those of châteaux Chasse-Spleen, Gressier Grand Poujeaux, Poujeaux and Maucaillou – have been ranged alongside the greatest of Bordeaux. Prices from these châteaux are generally higher than those from the rest of the village.

After the 1855 classification it was expected that Moulis wines would gradually win places amongst the classed growths. And in 1866 the local lawyer Bigeat wrote to the effect that the classification of a Moulis *cru* was only a matter of time. He could hardly have anticipated that practically nothing would ever change regarding the 1855 scheme.

LISTRAC-MEDOC

Listrac-Médoc, on the N215 (as with Moulis) has no *grand cru classé* châteaux, but it does have a communal appellation. As well as for some very celebrated châteaux, it is especially renowned for its energetically managed cooperative. Cave de Vinification de Listrac-Médoc, to use its official name, started in 1935 as a *cuverie* with a 5,000-hectolitre capacity – enormous in those days. Since 1948 the wine has gained quite a reputation as it is sold on French railways. Today, its capacity is nearly 30,000 hectolitres.

Within the commune boundaries here, there are three famous small gravel hills: at Fonréaud, Fourcas and Listrac itself. Listrac's reaches a height of 43 metres, making it the Médoc's highest point and the site of a fire tower. Listrac's subsoil is made up of layers of clay, lime and gravel. For

many years Merlot was the most important grape variety to grow on it, but at most wine estates you now find at least 50 per cent Cabernet Sauvignon. This has increased the finesse of the wines, as Listracs used to have a rather negative, rustic image. Although that has now changed and they are still virile, firm structured, very substantial wines. A pleasant white wine is now made at Château Fonréaud, the only Listrac estate to do so.

The village itself clusters around a small 13th-century church with an interesting spire. The original name, Listrac, was altered to Listrac-Médoc in 1986 to avoid possible confusion with Lirac in the Rhône region.

LISTRAC-MEDOC

HOTEL

Château Cap Léon Veyrin
T: 05 56 58 07 28, F: 05 56 58 07 50
Rooms and *table d'hôte* meals are available at this wine estate, but have to be booked. Prices of rooms from FF280.

RESTAURANTS

Château Rose Ste-Croix
T: 05 56 58 08 68
Small, simple restaurant, run by a winegrower's family. Regional specialities. The cheapest menu is under FF100. Some *chambres d'hôte*.

RECOMMENDED PRODUCERS

Château Clarke
Cru Bourgeois
T: 05 56 88 88 00, F: 05 56 58 26 46
Created by Baron Edmund de Rothschild. Also makes white wine.

Château Fonréaud
Cru Bourgeois
T: 05 56 58 02 43, F: 05 56 58 04 33
Collection of antique wine utensils on show.

Château Fourcas Dupré
Cru Bourgeois
T: 05 56 58 01 07, F: 05 56 58 02 27

Château Fourcas-Hosten
Cru Bourgeois
T: 05 56 58 01 15, F: 05 56 58 06 73

Château Fourcas-Loubaney
T: 05 56 58 03 83
Worth discovering.

Château Lestage
Cru Bourgeois
T: 05 56 58 02 43
Visits by appointment.

Château Mayne-Lalande
Cru Bourgeois
T: 05 56 58 27 63, F: 05 56 58 22 41
Top quality Listrac-Médocs.

Château Peyredon Lagravette
Cru Bourgeois
T: 05 56 58 05 55, F: 05 56 58 05 50
Open every day except Sunday.

Above Grape-pickers make their way to the vineyards. The Médoc harvest usually takes place during September.
Left A large property in Moulis, Château Mauvesin, was built in 1853 by the Le Blanc family, which had owned the property since the mid-1600s.

MARGAUX

To get to Margaux from Moulis visitors have a choice of routes: you can either drive via the D105 or return to the D2 at Arcins and approach this classic vineyard area on the wandering wine route. Between Margaux and Moulis is the little village of Avensan. It belongs to Haut-Médoc, but makes wines closely resembling those of Margaux. There are two interesting châteaux here: Citran and de Villegeorge.

Within the Margaux appellation there are about 1,350 hectares of vineyard. These cover five different communes: firstly, Margaux itself, then Soussans, Cantenac, Arsac and Labarde. The vineyards may be disparate, but they do not spread as far as to include those mid-stream in the Gironde (opposite Margaux there are some islands in the river which also have vineyards). These are outside the Margaux appellation and their wines must be classified as Bordeaux and Bordeaux Supérieur.

The 1855 classification ascribed 21 *grands crus* to Margaux – more than to any other Médoc appellation. Also, all five

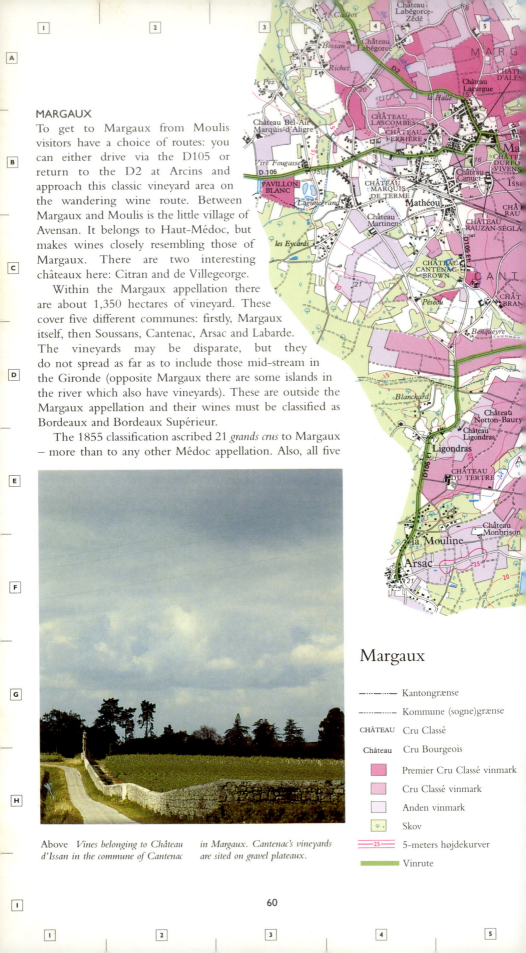

Above *Vines belonging to Château d'Issan in the commune of Cantenac in Margaux. Cantenac's vineyards are sited on gravel plateaux.*

Margaux

·—··—··—	Kantongrænse
·········—	Kommune (sogne)grænse
CHÂTEAU	Cru Classé
Château	Cru Bourgeois
▮	Premier Cru Classé vinmark
▮	Cru Classé vinmark
▯	Anden vinmark
▯	Skov
═25═	5-meters højdekurver
▬	Vinrute

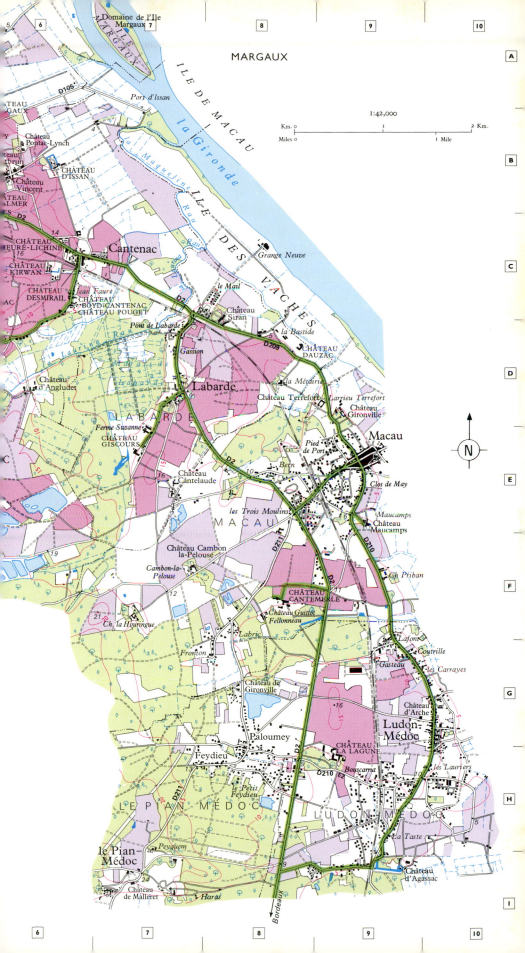

MARGAUX

Right A scenic corner of Château Cantemerle in the commune Macau (Haut-Médoc) of Margaux. This fifth-growth property is now producing exemplary wines since a change of ownership in 1980.

MARGAUX

RESTAURANTS AND HOTELS

Auberge de Savoie
T: 05 56 88 31 76
Congenial restaurant well-known for its very good value. Rural décor gives a pleasant atmosphere. Regional cuisine with modern presentation.
Le Pavillon de Margaux
T: 05 57 88 77 54, F: 05 57 88 77 73
Throughout the year, this is a nice small hotel to explore the Médoc from. Rooms start at around FF400. The restaurant is recommended too.
Relais de Margaux
T: 05 56 88 38 20
Don't be deterred by the luxurious surroundings, you can eat well and at fairly reasonable prices – sometimes in the company of château owners. Jazz brunches arranged on summer Sundays. There are luxurious rooms from about FF900.

RECOMMENDED PRODUCERS

AVENSAN
Château Citran
Cru Bourgeois
T: 05 56 58 21 01, F: 05 56 58 12 19
Much recent investment. A rich, harmonious Haut-Médoc with a complex, fruity, lingering aftertaste.
Château de Villegeorge
Cru Bourgeois
T: 05 57 88 70 20, F: 05 57 88 72 51
Broad, deep-coloured wine with fruity overtones and length. Ageing potential.

MARGAUX
Château Margaux
Grand Cru Classé (1er)
T: 05 57 88 70 28, F: 05 57 88 31 32
The most impressive château in the Médoc; a tree-lined avenue leads to a huge country house. One of the greatest wines in the world. Year in, year out it is of a magnificent quality, concentrated, wonderfully complex. The second wines, Pavillon Rouge and Blanc merit recommendation.
Château Lascombes
Grand Cru Classé (2ème)
T: 05 57 88 70 66, F: 05 57 88 72 17
Excellently managed estate (one of the Médoc's largest) with a château from 1904. Firm, elegant Margaux that develops well in bottle.

classes are represented in Margaux, which again is not an accolade awarded anywhere else. Such high quality in these wines is widely thought due to the fine composition of the soil. In Margaux this consists mainly of gravel brought down from the Massif Central and the Pyrenees in the Tertiary period. The soil is poorer than in other wine villages here. But poor soil usually gives a rich wine. The actual topsoil is thinner than elsewhere in the Médoc, the gravel content the highest, the microclimate the warmest, and production per hectare the lowest. In critiques, words such as 'elegant', 'feminine', 'subtle' and 'finesse' are used in describing Margaux's wines. These are not wines that reveal themselves quickly; you have to wait patiently before you can enjoy them. The rule of thumb is that a Margaux needs seven years before its qualities show to full advantage. But there are also firm, sturdier wines made here that demand even more

Château Malescot St-Exupéry
Grand Cru Classé (3ème)
T: 05 57 88 70 68, F: 05 57 88 35 80
This is a comfortable château, dating from 1885. Its scattered vineyards (some of them in Soussans) make balanced wine with colour, firmness, wood, and refinement. However the wines do need patience.

Château Marquis d'Alesme Becker
Grand Cru Classé (3ème)
T: 05 57 88 70 68, F: 05 57 88 35 80
The wine is elegant and strong, with supple tannin.

Château Marquis de Terme
Grand Cru Classé (4ème)
T: 05 57 88 30 01, F: 05 57 88 32 51
During the 1980s a great deal has been invested in equipment, cellars and reception rooms. The wine has benefited; it is firmly structured with deep colour, good fruit and tannin.

Château Rauzan-Ségla
Grand Cru Classé (2ème)
T: 05 57 88 70 30, F: 05 57 88 34 54
Older than most Médoc estates, the Rausan vineyards date back to 1661. Distinguished wine.

SOUSSANS
Château Labégorce
Cru Bourgeois
T: 05 57 88 71 32, F: 05 57 88 35 01
Renovated and revitalised. The result is an engaging wine full of fruit and rather fat.

Château Labégorce Zédé
T: 05 56 88 71 31, F: 05 57 88 72 54
Firm, award-winning, characterful, sound-structured wine.

Château Tayac
Cru Bourgeois
T: 05 57 88 33 06, F: 05 57 88 36 06
A pleasing wine with smooth fruity flavour.

time. They come mostly from vineyards in the west of the area, where the soil has rather more clay. The most northerly village in the Margaux group is Soussans. Not far from its centre is the site of Château La Tour de Mons, once a mighty castle. It was largely destroyed by fire in 1895, and only the remains of towers, a chapel and stables (now a cellar for bottles) still stand today.

Margaux itself is next on the route and is one of the world's best-known wine names, in part because of Château Margaux. This building, erected in 1815, has the aura of a palace and is immaculately maintained. And in its cellars – they are partly underground, which is not common in the Médoc – sublime wine is matured. Just to the side of the impressive château's drive stands Margaux's church, dating from the 18th century. The D2 makes a rather sudden left-angled turn into the village centre. At the end of the street you will see the Maison du Vin, where the fullest information about the appellation can be obtained.

There is also a large assortment of wines on sale. At Sprengnether's, the local *pâtissier*, the famous *Sarments du Médoc* – little chocolate vine branches – are made . Near the railway crossing, on the Arsac road, there is a small factory making wine cases. The lids of these cases marked with the château insignia make quite collectable items.

Leaving Margaux on the D2 travelling south, the next commune in the group is Cantenac. At its centre sits an 18th-century church

Above left *The peaceful village of Margaux.*
Left *A weathered statue in the grounds of Château Prieuré-Lichine.*

Château La Tour de Bessan
T: 05 57 88 83 33, F: 05 57 88 72 51
Attractive wine.

Château La Tour de Mons
Cru Bourgeois
T: 05 57 88 33 03, F: 05 57 88 32 46
Estate with remains of a 13th-century
castle. Deep-coloured, inaccessible in
youth, but develops well in bottle.

CANTENAC
Château d'Angludet
Cru Bourgeois
T: 05 57 88 71 41, F: 05 57 88 72 52
Sichel family makes a wine that shines,
with rich, complex aromas and taste.

Château Brane-Cantenac
Grand Cru Classé (2ème)
T: 05 57 88 70 20, F: 05 57 88 72 51
Large, well-run Lurton property with
prime vineyards on Cantenac's
plateau. Quality levels vary, but fruity
and elegant wines, good for ageing.

Château Cantenac-Brown
Grand Cru Classé (3ème)
T: 05 56 73 24 70, F: 05 57 88 81 90
Imposing building. Powerful,
well-balanced wine.

Château Desmirail
Grand Cru Classé (3ème)
T: 05 57 88 34 33, F: 05 57 88 72 51
The Brane-Cantenac team makes the
wine, now back on the scene. Today,
it is a stylish wine with great finesse.

Château d'Issan
Grand Cru Classé (3ème)
T: 05 57 88 35 91, F: 05 57 88 74 24
Boasts a 17th-century moated
château, one of the most splendid
sights in the Médoc. The wine is
elegant with lovely aromas of red
berry fruit and supple tannins.

Château Kirwan
Grand Cru Classé (3ème)
T: 05 57 88 71 42, F: 05 57 88 77 62
An 18th-century manor house with a
beautiful show of flowers in summer.
Elegant wine with potential to mature.

with an octagonal tower and a fine interior well worth exploring. Here, too, is Château Prieuré-Lichine, a former monastery with grounds tastefully converted into a wine estate. It has a reception centre where visitors are welcome every day of the year, and a video about winegrowing is shown. To conclude your tour you are given a glass of wine. Ranged around the village of Cantenac are a number of châteaux, including d'Issan, surrounded by a moat. There is a wine shop in Cantenac, but prices are neither higher nor lower than anywhere else.

To the east of the village, Cantenac's gravel plateaux leads on to pastures and water meadows, or *palus*. Further away, where the D209 and D2 roads intersect near a railway crossing, is the tiny settlement of Labarde. Labarde belongs to the Margaux appellation. It has an 18th-century church housing a carved wooden main altar. Within Labarde some excellent wines are made at châteaux such as Giscours (thriving again thanks to a dynamic Dutch owner), Siran (a *cru bourgeois* with the distinction of a *cru classé*) and Dauzac (restored to former glory).

Westwards from Cantenac, a narrow road winds through vineyards and woods towards minuscule Arsac – the southernmost

Margaux commune. On a low hill just outside this village stands the wholly renovated Château du Tertre, a fifth-growth *grand cru classé*. Château d'Arsac, on the other hand, has perhaps the most unorthodox frontage of any in the Médoc: all its wooden window frames and doors are painted a light blue colour. The building has an impressive setting in a fine park. The winemaking equipment here is modern, and there is a visitors' centre with exhibitions of modern art, which is open daily.

Château Palmer
Grand Cru Classé (3ème)
T: 05 57 88 72 72, F: 05 57 88 37 16
Picture-book château with its four pointed towers. Among the very best Médoc wines: stylish suppleness, great refinement and perfect balance.

Château Prieuré-Lichine
Grand Cru Classé (4ème)
T: 05 57 88 36 28, F: 05 57 88 78 93
Probably the most hospitable Grand Cru in the Médoc. Former monastery. Today, the wine is well-balanced, and fairly elegant with decent tannin. Gains in richness and class in classic years.

ARSAC
Château d'Arsac
T: 05 56 58 83 90, F: 05 56 58 83 08
Hospitable, dynamic, modern estate: cellars in striking blue. Art exhibitions.

Château du Tertre
Grand Cru Classé (5ème)
T: 05 56 59 30 08, F: 05 56 59 71 51
Carefully restored building on a low hill. The only *grand cru classé* here: excellent, elegant Margaux. Owned by the same Dutch family of Château Giscours.

LABARDE
Château Dauzac
Grand Cru Classé (5ème)
T: 05 57 88 32 10, F: 05 57 88 96 00
Almost total renewal and renovation has led to a quality wine with plenty of aromas and complex, elegant length.

Château Giscours
Grand Cru Classé (3ème)
T: 05 57 97 09 09, F: 05 57 97 09 00
Huge rambling château and *chais* in a fine park. Reliable wine with an intense palate, fine colour, and lingering tannins.

Château Siran
T: 05 57 88 34 04, F: 05 57 88 70 05
Wines maturing in the nuclear-proof cellar here are charmingly rounded, full of finesse and pedigree.

Above *Fertilizing and spraying in the vineyard are carried out judiciously, using preparations which are as natural as possible.*
Left *The imposing moated third growth Château d'Issan is one of the most spectacular sights in the Médoc.*
Far left *First growth Château Margaux, a beautiful country maison.*

MACAU

RESTAURANTS

Chez Quinquin
T: 05 57 88 45 89
On a terrace by the Gironde, this is a good, inexpensive place specialising in fish dishes. Attractive view over river.

La Guinguette
T: 05 56 30 08 12
Next to Chez Quinquin. Lots of *fruits de mer*. Sunday lunch for about FF130.

RECOMMENDED PRODUCERS

Château Cambon La Pelouse
Cru Bourgeois
T: 05 57 88 40 32, F: 05 57 88 19 12
Charming wine with length, usually drinkable within two years of vintage.

Château Cantemerle
Grand Cru Classé (5ème)
T: 05 57 97 02 82, F: 05 57 97 02 84
Fairy-tale château hidden in romantic woods. Very good wine since 1980s: concentrated, complex, fine tannins.

Château Lescalle
T: 05 57 88 07 64, F: 05 57 88 07 00
Bordeaux Supérieur
Rounded taste of bilberries and supple tannin. Has potential for keeping. Made by the Château Maucamps team.

Château Maucamps
Cru Bourgeois
T: 05 57 88 07 64, F: 05 57 88 07 00
This château makes great wine and has a growing reputation – elegant and pure.

LUDON

RESTAURANTS

Le Petit Bacalan
T: 05 56 30 32 11
Unpretentious country cuisine. Reasonable prices.

MACAU

From Labarde you can drive via the D209 or the D2 to Macau. Macau is a village with some 2,600 inhabitants. It also has a partly Romanesque church with a fine belltower. Apart from this it is hardly worth a visit; but in the immediate neighbourhood there are a few places that, for various reasons, merit a small detour. The first of these is on the D2, the fifth growth *grand cru classé* Château Cantemerle, with perhaps the finest set of railings in the whole Médoc. They enclose an impressive park. Just outside the village, near the Ludon road, is Château Maucamps, a large estate of nearly 60 hectares – about 20 of which are vineyard. This produces a Haut-Médoc wine with a reputation that has been growing steadily since 1981; the number of medals won at the various French wine *concours* is mounting up nicely.

Macau's little harbour on the Gironde used to be worthy of note; but although the signboard saying 'Port' is a reminder of this, decline has clearly set in. Near the water there is a pleasant *guinguette*, a small tavern and garden. This is a lovely spot to spend a relaxing few hours – especially in

summer and certainly for lunch, when simple and good-tasting fish dishes are on the menu. From the harbour, a road runs south along an embankment, with vineyards to the right. Among them are those of Château Lescalle, which has the same owner as Château Maucamps. Château Lescalle, however, is not entitled to the Haut-Médoc appellation and is a Bordeaux Supérieur.

LUDON

From Macau it is just a short drive to Ludon, a little to the south. Ludon itself is a sleepy commuters' village, around a church, built in various styles. An interesting collection of old winemaking equipment can be seen at Château d'Arche in the centre. Close to the D2 heading out of Ludon is Château La Lagune, the southernmost *grand cru classé* in the Médoc. The road there, which runs parallel to the D2, leads past Ludon's most important place of interest, Château d'Agassac. This is a weathered castle built in the 13th century on the foundations of an earlier feudal stronghold. The *seigneur* of Agassac was a thriftless gentleman who became involved in a scandal: one morning a servant was found dead in the château's moat. The *seigneur* was regarded as responsible but the whole affair was covered up. In the 16th century the castle passed into the hands of the Pomiès, a family which produced some well-known political figures. The present owner is the firm Groupama.

Above *Part of the immense Landes forest near Lac de Lacenau, just west of the Médoc.*
Above left *The Lion d'Or in Arcins, one of the most popular restaurants in the Médoc.*
Far left *Barrel-making in the village of Ludon, near Margaux.*

RECOMMENDED PRODUCERS

Château La Lagune
T: 05 57 88 44 07
The 1730 château was originally a Carthusian monastery. Reliable, firm wine: well-balanced, mellow firmness, with a hint of vanilla from new casks.

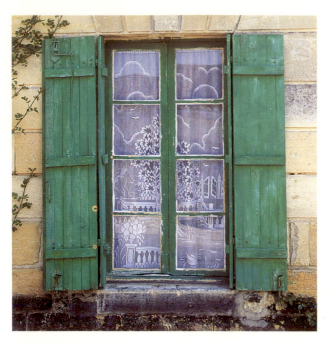

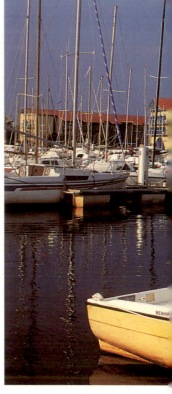

SOUTHERN HAUT-MEDOC

RECOMMENDED PRODUCERS

Château Clément-Pichon
Cru Bourgeois (Parempuyre)
T: 05 56 35 23 79, F: 05 56 35 85 23
Since 1977 wine has once again been made here with great success after the estate had lain fallow for nearly 60 years. This is a good Haut-Médoc with traces of new wood in its aftertaste.

Château Dillon
Cru Bourgeois (Blanquefort)
T: 05 56 35 56 35, F: 05 56 95 36 75
The wine from the local agricultural school; easy to drink and showing typical characteristics. Exhibition of Erik Dietmann's *'Les gardiens des barriques'* (large noses) is on permanent display.

Above *In contrast to the grandeur of the Bordeaux châteaux, a simple village home in Haut-Médoc.*
Below *The Abbey at La Réole (Entre-Deux-Mers).*

HAUT-MEDOC: THE SOUTHERN EXTREME

As you drive south from Ludon you head towards the end of the classic Médoc wine route. One of the last places you will come to is Parempuyre (just east of the D2). Despite its location, it is still well worth the visit. It has a 19th-century church with paintings of the same period. One of Bordeaux's biggest wine firms is established in the village: CVBG, which owns brands like Dourthe Frères and Kressmann. Next to it is the entrance to the wholly restored Château Clément-Pichon; the drive cuts through the vineyard.

Next you will reach Blanquefort. Like most places on the outskirts of Bordeaux, Blanquefort consists of a jumble of

dwellings in every possible style. According to legend, the local castle (with a moat, six towers and a keep) is protected by the ghost of the Black Prince. In Blanquefort there is a school of agriculture and winegrowing (*lycée agricole*), which runs Château Dillon, its own estate. In the well-designed *chai* there is a permanent exhibition of 21 large 'noses'. This collection was bought by the French Ministry of Culture and then loaned to the school.

Above *The pier at Hourtin. The coast is just a few kilometres away from most Bordeaux vineyards.*
Left *Fruit on display in one of the local markets. Try serving fresh fruit such as melon with a glass of young Sauternes or Barsac.*

Château Magnol
Cru Bourgeois (Blanquefort)
T: 05 56 95 48 00, F: 05 56 95 48 01
Belongs to the large wine firm, Barton & Guestier, and makes an attractive Haut-Médoc with power.

Château du Taillan
Cru Bourgeois (Le Taillan-Médoc)
T: 05 56 95 14 07, F: 05 56 35 87 49
Beautiful park and historical cellars. A clean, elegant red wine and a pleasant white, Château La Dame Blanche.

These 'noses' represent 'the custodians of good wine'. From Blanquefort, you could make a short detour to Le Taillan, just to the west, and visit the splendid Château du Taillan. In addition to its red Haut-Médoc, a white Bordeaux, Château La Dame Blanche, is produced here. White wines are rare in the Médoc, but more and more producers are planting white grapes besides black varieties.

Graves and Sauternes

South of Bordeaux stretches a large winegrowing area that is divided into several very well-known appellations: Pessac-Léognan, Graves and Sauternes, to name just three. This is an area with a great diversity of wines. In the Graves district both red and white wines are produced; in Sauternes, the range is all white, with dry, semi-sweet or *moelleux* to choose from. The grape varieties blended to make them are Cabernet Sauvignon, Cabernet Franc and Merlot for the reds, and Sauvignon, Sémillon and Muscadelle for the whites.

Besides simple semi-sweet Graves Supérieurs and other basic wines, the area also produces reds and whites of high quality – of interest to every enthusiast. The Maison des Vins de Graves in Podensac offers valuable help in describing them: records and literature are good, there is a *vinothèque*, and the visitor is given a friendly and hospitable welcome, added to which the office is open all year round. There are about 100 châteaux in the area and apart from those in Pessac-Léognan, where it is customary to make an appointment, the estates are open practically every day to visitors. In many cases English is spoken.

The Graves district extends southeast past the town of Langon, interrupted by the vineyards of Cérons, Sauternes and Barsac, enclaves with their own appellations. The landscape in this part of the Bordeaux region is well worth exploring; the environs of Labrède, where Montesquieu's castle stands, are particularly beautiful. The Sauternes district, with its many châteaux, is just as picturesque. There are many spots in the Graves where you can enjoy a fine view of the wine districts on the opposite bank of the Garonne.

Left The stunning, moated Château de La Brède, the birthplace and home of the famous statesman, politician and writer, Montesquieu. The castle dates partly from the 13th century.

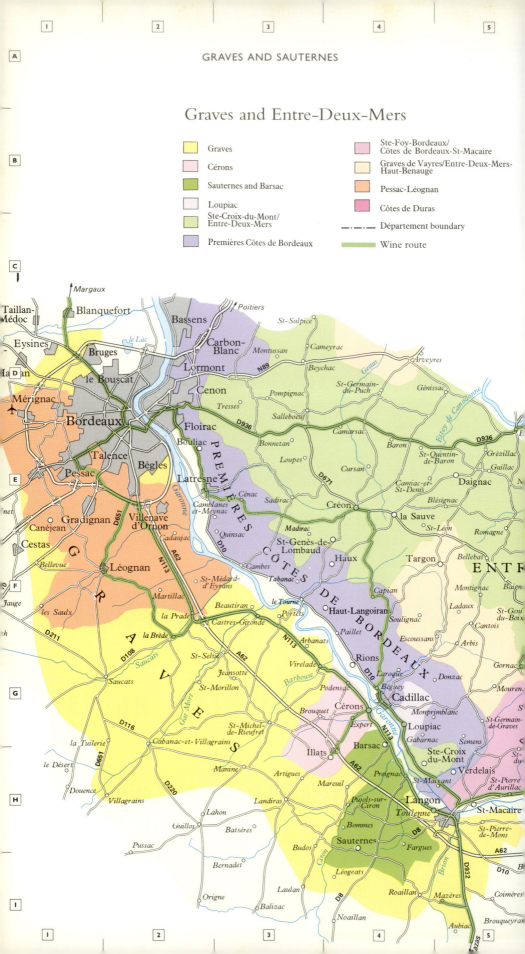

Graves and Entre-Deux-Mers

Graves

Cérons

Sauternes and Barsac

Loupiac
Ste-Croix-du-Mont/
Entre-Deux-Mers

Premières Côtes de Bordeaux

Ste-Foy-Bordeaux/
Côtes de Bordeaux-St-Macaire

Graves de Vayres/Entre-Deux-Mers-
Haut-Benauge

Pessac-Léognan

Côtes de Duras

Département boundary

Wine route

Graves

The southern suburbs

If you could transport yourself back in time to the Middle Ages, you would see Bordeaux as a walled city, wholly centred on quayside activities along the River Garonne. Just to the south, the city was fringed by a semi-circle of parishes: Saint-Genès, Talence, Pessac and Bègles. These made up 'Graves de Bordeaux', the city's original winegrowing district. At this time, wine was already one of the region's major exports.

Today you must search amongst office blocks to find the vineyards, in so far as they still exist. Bègles is best known now for its rugby club, and Talence for its university – but the latter redeems itself a little as home of the Institut d'Oenologie. The construction of the Mérignac airport also meant uprooting vines; a tiny vineyard near the perimeter has been kept as homage to the grape; for the rest it is all asphalt and concrete.

1:300,000

PESSAC-LEOGNAN

HOTELS

La Réserve
74 Avenue du Bourgailh (Alouette)
T: 05 56 07 13 28, F: 05 57 26 58 00
Luxurious rooms from around FF600,
swimming pool, tennis courts; good,
classic cuisine: set menus from FF190.

Hôtel Guyenne
Avenue François-Rabelais (Talence)
T: 05 56 80 75 08, F: 05 56 84 48 60
Pleasant hotel owned by the popular
Lycée Hôtelier. Closed school holidays.

RESTAURANTS

Les Chasseurs
Tel: 05 56 64 11 58 (Léognan)
Village restaurant, set lunch from FF85.

Grill La Forge
T: 05 56 64 11 58 (Léognan)
Good for a quick bite, from FF80.

Le Châlet Lyrique
T: 05 56 89 11 59, F: 05 56 89 53 37
(Gradignan)
Pleasant hotel/restaurant. Spacious,
comfortable rooms from FF350. Meat
dishes prevail as the owner was once
a butcher. Set menus from FF200.

RECOMMENDED PRODUCERS

Château Bouscaut
Cru Classé
T: 05 57 96 01 26, F: 05 57 96 01 27
(Cadaujac)
Splendid 18th-century estate. Since
1980, a Lurton property. Aromatic,
fresh white with a taste that lingers.

Château Haut-Brion
Grand Cru Classé (1er) (red)
T: 05 56 00 29 30, F: 05 56 98 75 14
(Pessac)
The only Graves estate to be included
in the 1855 classification. The large 16th-
century château used to be beyond
the Bordeaux town boundary, but is
now surrounded by suburbs. Noble,
velvet-smooth red wine with sublime
balance and long, gratifying aftertaste.
Distinguished, long-lived white.

PESSAC

Typical of post-World War II development is the situation in Pessac, where such renowned châteaux as Haut-Brion, La Mission Haut-Brion, Les Carmes Haut-Brion and Pape Clément are surrounded by flats and other dwellings. What happened at Château Les Carmes Haut-Brion is rather remarkable. The vineyard of this seven-hectare estate is surrounded by a wall (which has perhaps saved it from all the urban expansion). It now appears, however, that the houses around this vineyard provide it with extra protection, giving rise to a different, warmer microclimate. The grapes at Château Les Carmes Haut-Brion often ripen earlier than elsewhere in Pessac.

Château Haut-Brion is the first name that springs to mind when mentioning Pessac and is probably the first *grand cru* to be exported out of the region. In 1664, Samuel Pepys, the diarist and *bon vivant*, wrote that he had tasted 'Ho Bryan, a wine of a new style and distinctive taste', at the Royal Oak tavern in London's Lombard Street. Haut-Brion had already been in existence for more than a century by then. Its founder, Jean de Pontac, had begun in 1530 to buy up plots around his '*maison noble*' and gradually pieced them together into a vineyard. Château Haut-Brion was the only Graves wine to be admitted into the *grands crus classés* in the 1855 classification.

On August 7th 1953 a first semi-official ranking of the Graves *crus* was published. More important recognition came on September 9th 1987, when the Pessac-Léognan *appellation contrôlée* was granted. There are ten communities in the suburbs and around the outskirts of Bordeaux that are entitled to this: Cadaujac, Canéjan, Gradignan, Léognan, Martillac, Mérignac, Pessac, Saint-Médard-d'Eyrans, Talence, and Villenave d'Ornon. Of these communes, Léognan, Martillac and Pessac are by far the most important.

LEOGNAN

The easiest way to get from Pessac to Léognan is via the ring road, leaving it at exit 18. Turn right immediately afterwards and then bear left when the road forks – this is the D651 which will take you right there. Léognan is one of the ten places that make up the Pessac-Léognan appellation and, with some 425 hectares of vineyards, it is its most important.

Léognan has about 20 of the 55 or so châteaux in Pessac-Léognan. Fifteen produce both red and white wines. One of the smallest estates in the whole of Bordeaux is to be found here: Domaine du Petit Bourdieu, with just 0.75 hectares and an average yield of 3,000 bottles of red wine a year.

The village itself does not perhaps amount to much, but it does have a Romanesque church (restored in the 19th century). In the centre is a wine shop, the Caves de Léognan, located next to the cellars of Château Malartic-Lagravière.

To start your tour of the Léognan and Martillac châteaux you should drive from the centre of the village up to the churchyard. Here the road to the left leads to Le Bouscat. By going right, then first left (onto the D109), you will come to Martillac. This route is highly recommended as it gives you a good view of the very gravelly soil (the *graves*), and the

Château Pape Clément
Cru Classé
T: 05 56 07 04 11, F: 05 56 07 36 70
(Pessac)
Established in 1300 by Archbishop Bertrand de Goth of Bordeaux, later Pope Clement V. Red wine with a broad, generous taste and strong constitution. White is less impressive.

Château La Mission Haut-Brion
Cru Classé
T: 05 56 00 29 30, F: 05 56 98 75 14
(Talence)
Dark red wine of high quality. Same owners as Château Haut-Brion.

Château Carbonnieux
Cru Classé
T: 05 56 87 08 28, F: 05 56 87 52 18
(Léognan)
Famous old estate, taken over by Benedictine monks in 1741 – they exported their white wine to the (Muslim) Turkish court as 'mineral water'. Pale white wine with a clean, fresh taste. The red needs ageing.

Château de Fieuzal
Cru Classé
T: 05 56 64 77 86, F: 05 56 64 18 88
(Léognan)
One of the district's best red wines. Plenty of fruit, tannin and a long finish. The white wine is at least as good.

Château de France
T: 05 56 64 75 39, F: 05 56 64 72 13
(Léognan)
Decent red wine with deep colour and a powerful aftertaste. The white is agreeable, fruity and oaked.

Château Haut-Bailly
Cru Classé
T: 05 56 64 75 11, F: 05 56 64 53 47
(Léognan) An unspectacular-looking château making an almost satiny red wine of outstanding quality.

Château Larrivet Haut-Brion
T: 05 56 64 75 51, F: 05 56 64 53 47
(Léognan)
Fragrant, fresh white wine. Structured red, needing some maturing.

Château Malartic-Lagravière
Cru Classé
T: 05 56 64 75 08, F: 05 56 64 53 66
(Léognan)
Pleasing fresh white with a long, generous finish. The red, with deep colour and character, needs keeping.

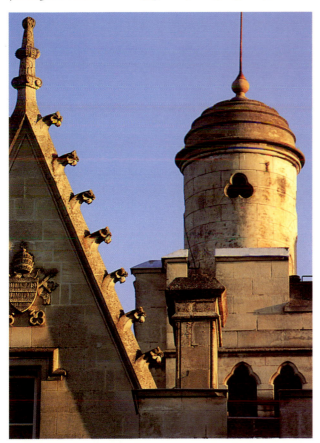

Far left (top) *Immaculate vines belonging to Château Haut-Brion.*
Far left (below) *Old steps at Château Olivier, a medieval moated fortress with a gravelly vineyard.*
Left *Château Pape Clément, a handsome property established in 1300.*

lie of the vineyards. A wine route, a *circuit touristique des crus classés*, has been set out, but the signposting in places leaves something to be desired. Two of the most visually attractive properties awaiting discovery here are Château La Louvière, built at the end of the 18th century by Victor Louis, the famous architect of Bordeaux's Grand Théâtre; and Château Olivier, a medieval stronghold with a moat around it. Quite a few estates are open to visitors; in many cases, though, it is advisable to make an appointment beforehand. For a good meal many winegrowers prefer a restaurant in Gradignan.

MARTILLAC

When you drive from Léognan to Martillac (take the D109), you see before you a great expanse of wine district. After an action group – led by André Lurton – managed to stop valuable gravel soils being sacrificed to projects other than wine, the extension of the Martillac vineyards began. There

Above *It is worth visiting Château Olivier, even if only to appreciate the* *fairytale-like Middle Age* *splendour of this moated fortress.*

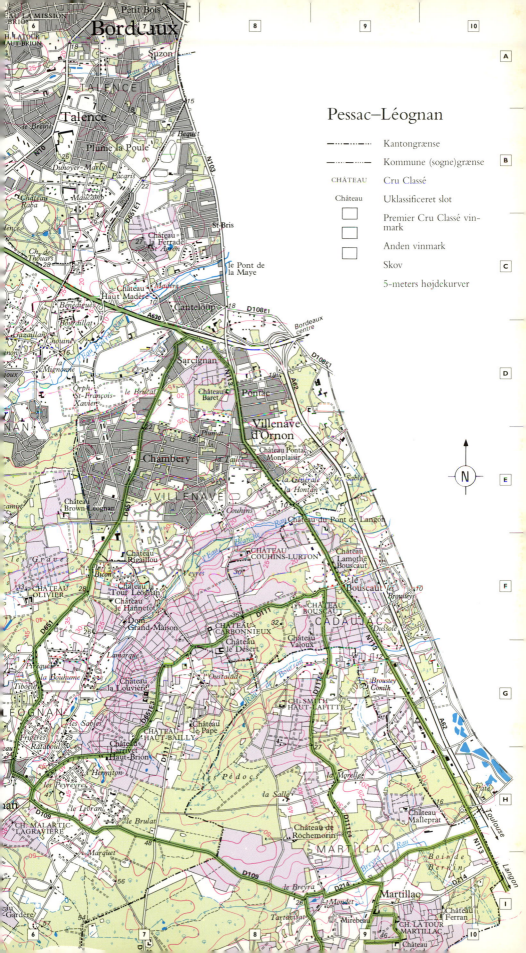

Pessac–Léognan

·—··—··—··	Kantongrænse
—·—·—·—	Kommune (sogne)grænse
CHÂTEAU	Cru Classé
Château	Uklassificeret slot
▢	Premier Cru Classé vin-mark
▢	Anden vinmark
▢	Skov
	5-meters højdekurver

Château Olivier
Cru Classé
T: 05 56 64 73 31, F: 05 56 64 54 23
(Léognan)
The château is a splendid medieval,
moated fortress. Gravelly vineyards
give fresh, clean white; elegant red.

Domaine de Chevalier
Cru Classé
T: 05 56 64 16 16, F: 05 56 64 18 18
(Léognan)
This is a remarkable vineyard – in a
clearing deep in the woods behind
the village. It makes magnificent
white wine that surpasses almost
all other dry white Bordeaux, and
it is made with meticulous attention

to detail. The red is also excellent,
tending to a great Médoc in
personality.

MARTILLAC

 RESTAURANT

Hostellerie Lou Pistou
T: 05 56 23 71 02
Although it doesn't look as if it would
be from the outside, the cooking
here is good. Menus for under FF100.

 RECOMMENDED PRODUCERS

Château La Garde
T: 05 56 72 71 07, F: 05 56 72 66 36
(Martillac)
Pleasant red wine, harmonious and
refined in its flavours. The same is
true of the white.

Château La Tour Martillac
Cru Classé
T: 05 56 72 71 21, F: 05 56 72 64 03
(Martillac)
This is an unassuming château with

*Above and far right Two aspects
of the charming town of Bazas, near
Langon: a Bazadaise cow and one
of the town's many beautiful streets.
Right Grapes in traditional leather
paniers at Château Pape-Clément.*

is now substantial investment in viticulture here, and it is safe
to assume that some wines of surprising quality will emerge.
Martillac has quite an elevated situation – rare in this region.

In the village there is a Romanesque church with some
interesting painted reliefs. A little way from the centre is the
Château La Tour Martillac, dating from 1750 and with a
tower even older in its courtyard. More or less facing it is
Château La Garde, with newly built cellars under the lawns.

LABREDE

Charles Louis de Segondat, Baron de la Brède et de
Montesquieu, was born at the castle of La Brède in 1689.
Thanks to this French philosopher, writer (*L'Esprit des Lois*
and *Lettres Persanes*), member of parliament
and mayor of Bordeaux, the name of the
village – and his own in the shortened form
Montesquieu – have remained well-known.
The virtually unspoiled Gothic castle (dating
from the 13th and 15th centuries) has an
especially beautiful setting. It stands in a
moat and is surrounded by woods,
meadows and vineyards. There is said to be
an underground passage from the castle to
Château de Rochemorin, which also
belonged to Montesquieu. The castle is open

for visiting at weekends. His library there, with some 7,000 volumes, is still intact. The little village of Labrède, which borders on the Martillac district, has 100 hectares of vineyard, 80 per cent of which is occupied by two producers.

PODENSAC AND ITS ENVIRONS

The A62 motorway divides the Graves area into two. The district south of Labrède, with its low-lying landscape of woods, meadows and maize fields, is of scant interest to the wine-lover. However, if you drive from Labrède on this motorway, or take the N113 *route nationale*, you will come to more interesting surroundings with wine villages such as Castres, Portets, and Podensac.

The most important sight to see in Portets is the Château de Portets, built in the 19th century on the foundations of a much older fortification. The château stands at the centre of a large park and has, as its entrance, an impressive wrought-iron gate (which appears on the wine labels). The village name derives from the word '*port*' – the harbour here used to handle considerable quantities of goods for export. Another sight worth exploring is the 18th–century Château de Mongeau, where there is a museum devoted to Waldec de Lessart, Louis XVI's last minister of foreign affairs.

Podensac has the excellent and helpful Maison du Vin de Graves. If you are travelling in the area you should really try

an old tower (the remains of a 12th-century fort) in the inner courtyard. The white is a classic dry Graves, improved with bottle age.

Château Smith Haut Lafitte
Cru Classé
T: 05 56 30 72 30, F: 05 56 03 96 26 (Martillac)
Remarkable, fairly recent château and cellar complex amidst the vineyards. Both the white and red Pessac-Léognan wines seem to improve every vintage. On the premises are a beauty farm and an excellent restaurant, *Aux Sources de Caudalie*. This is run by a talented chef and his wife, one of France's top *sommeliers*. (Tel: 05 57 83 11 26.) Also the château itself runs a small luxurious hotel with double rooms from about FF1,100.

LABREDE

RESTAURANTS

La Maison des Graves
T: 05 56 20 06 40
Restaurant in the centre of the village with fairly modern cuisine that includes *Saumon en Infusion de Graves*. Excellent list with many unfamiliar wines. Set menus from about FF100.

RECOMMENDED PRODUCERS

Château Magneau
T: 05 56 20 20 57, F: 05 56 20 39 95
Full-bodied, refined white Graves that is soon ready for drinking. The red wine is firm, with fruit.

IN AND AROUND PODENSAC

RESTAURANTS

Le Bel Ombrage
T: 05 56 67 01 66 (Castres)
A simple restaurant with reasonable cooking. Set menus start around FF65.
Relais des Trois Mousquetaires
T: 05 56 27 09 07 (Podensac)
Relaxed restaurant with good cooking. Classic regional dishes and a choice of three set menus all around FF100, each of them starting with soup.
Ma Vie La
T: 05 56 27 07 24 (Portets)
On the village square. Simple, but good and surprisingly inexpensive food (oysters, salads and *grillades*).

RECOMMENDED PRODUCERS

Château de Chantegrive
T: 05 56 27 17 38, F: 05 56 27 29 42
(Podensac)
Juicy red wine with distinct oaky
notes. The white comes from older
vines and has a complex bouquet and
a good fresh taste.

Château Cheret-Pitres
T&F: 05 56 67 27 76
(Portets)
Near the river (to get here take the
road to Langoiran). Deep-coloured,
smoky red Graves packed with juice
and fruit.

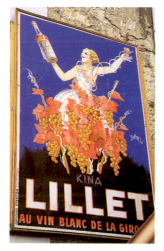

Château Rahoul
T: 05 56 67 01 12, F: 05 56 67 02 88
(Portets)
Outstanding white wine with a
nuanced taste and a smooth, refined
finish. The red, too, has style and
distinction.

Château de Landiras
T: 05 56 62 44 70, F: 05 56 62 43 78
(Landiras)
Castle ruin (14th century) with cellars
where a rich white, and a balanced
red Graves are produced. You can
also taste here the fine wines of
Domaine La Grave.

Main picture *This pretty house
is in the village of Portets, which
produces some notable Graves wines.*
Above *The local sweet vermouth,
Lillet, is a surprisingly good and
reasonably priced foil to foie gras.*
Far right (top) *Château La
Mission Haut-Brion.*

to visit it. There is also a well-stocked *vinothèque* where
Pessac-Léognan wines are amongst those for sale.

Podensac also boasts its own wine-based aperitif, Lillet,
and a related factory (in the main street) with an attractive
museum that includes old posters and labels. Visitors are
welcome and while there they can taste a glass of Lillet. It is
also worth spending time in the Parc de Chavat where there
is a remarkable sculpture collection.

CERONS

In the southern part of the Graves there are three districts
with their own appellations. They are surrounded on all
sides by the Graves and share its geological structure. These
districts are Cérons, Barsac and Sauternes.

The small area around the village of Cérons is a
transitional zone between Graves and Sauternes: here the
four most important wines of the two areas – namely red,
dry white, semi-sweet and sweet white – are all made. This
means that various appellations are in use. The red and the
dry white wines are sold as Graves, the semi-sweet whites as

Graves Supérieures, and the sweet as Cérons. (*Botrytis cinerea*, or 'noble rot', responsible for the lusciously sweet *vins liquoreux* occurs here, but a little less alluringly, perhaps, than further south in the famed appellations of Barsac and Sauternes.)

As early as the 3rd century AD there was mention of wines from '*Sirione*', and the name has ended up as Cérons. The old centre of this town lies between the N113 and the River Garonne. There is a 12th-century Romanesque church here, which has been later extended and enlarged. Opposite it stands Château de Cérons, built about three centuries ago by the Marquis de Calvimont. On the east side of the N113 is the village square, with an old market hall. The Syndicat Viticole – which in 1921 achieved the granting of the Cérons appellation – is here also.

Illats, also under Cérons jurisdiction, has an interesting 12th-century Romanesque church with a fine interior.

Vieux Château Gaubert
T & F: 05 56 67 52 76 (Portets)
Tasting cellar and castle ruins. Very successful, almost masterly dry white wine, and refined, pure-tasting red.

CERONS

HOTEL

La Grappe d'Or
T: 05 56 27 11 61
Simple hotel on the village square. Prices from around FF235. Has an unpretentious restaurant.

RECOMMENDED PRODUCERS

Château de Cérons
T: 05 56 27 01 13, F: 05 56 27 22 17 (Cérons)
Sound, sweet white wine from a relatively small estate. The dry white Graves is Château de Calvimont.

Château Lamouroux
T: 05 56 27 01 53, F: 05 56 27 08 86 (Cérons)
A generous white Graves with a full, flavourful aftertaste. Also the source of one of the better Cérons wines, Grand Enclos du Château de Cérons.

Château d'Archambeau
T: 05 56 62 51 46, F: 05 56 62 47 98 (Illats)
White wine with lovely pure fruit; supple-tasting, deep-coloured reds; powerful Cérons.

Château d'Ardennes
T: 05 56 62 53 80, F: 05 56 62 43 67 (Illats)
The red has good depth of colour, with supple meatiness and juicy fruit. The white is creamy with an agreeable, fruity, rounded taste.

Château d'Arricaud
T: 05 56 62 51 29, F: 05 56 62 41 47 (Landiras)
Semi-sweet Graves Supérieures with a good deal of breeding, which also applies to the dry white and the red.

Sauternes and Barsac

The wines

About 25 kilometres south of Bordeaux there is a small district that produces one of the world's most amazing wines – Sauternes. Sauternes wines were included in the 1855 classification and were the only Bordeaux whites to be given this honour. But despite such an accolade and although wine had been made there for hundreds of years, fame had not yet truly arrived. It was not until 1859 that the great international breakthrough began. In 1859, Russian Grand Duke Constantine visited Château d'Yquem and tasted a 12 year-old wine (1847 vintage). He was so impressed by it that he offered 20,000 gold francs for a *tonneau* (1,200 bottles). Made from late-picked grapes which had rotted in a quite remarkable way the wine from Château d'Yquem had therefore not been put on the market.

The secret of Sauternes lies in its micro-climate. In the autumn, cold water flows from the Ciron and other streams into the much warmer Garonne River, creating a morning mist that leaves a moist film on the grapes: the ideal growing medium for *Botrytis cinerea*, a tiny fungus

Sauternes and Barsac

---·---·---·---	Canton boundary
------·------	Commune (parish) boundary
CHÂTEAU	Cru Classé
Château	Cru Bourgeois
▮	Premier Grand Cru Classé vineyard
▯	Other vineyard
▯	Woods
〜50〜	Contour interval 5 metres
▬▬▬	Wine route

1:41,500

Km. 0 ———— 1 ———— 2 Km.
Miles 0 ———— 1 Mile

Below Vines near the village of Pujols-sur-Ciron. Mists rising from the Ciron stream provide the perfect damp conditions for the development of Botrytis cinerea on warm, early autumn days.

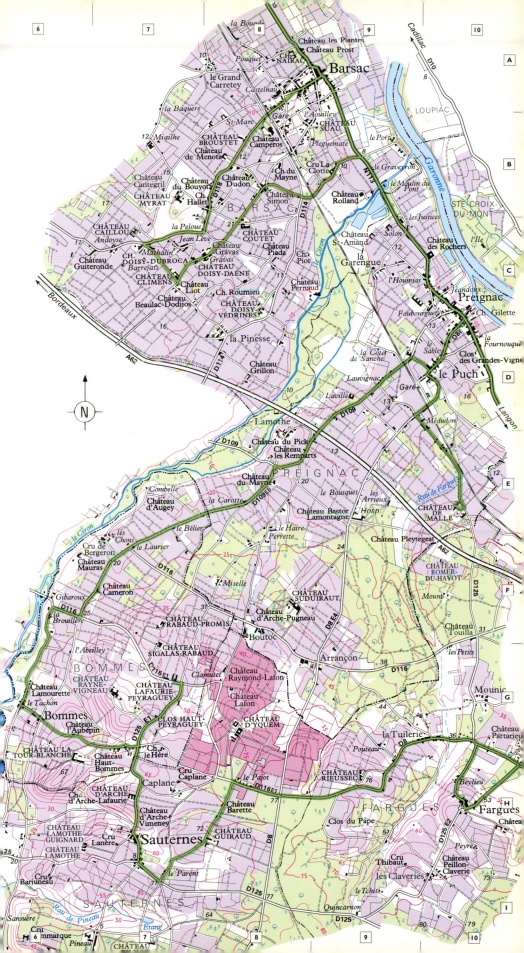

SAUTERNES AND BARSAC

HOTELS

Château de Valmont
T: 05 56 27 28 24, F: 05 56 27 17 53
(Barsac)
Former wine estate, now 200 years
old. Above what was the cellar are
12 rooms all with excellent
bathrooms. Each room is named
after a château, a small bottle of
whose wine welcomes the guests.
The rooms are quiet, despite the
popularity of this hotel for weddings,
etc. Prices from about FF500. At
night it runs a good restaurant.

RESTAURANTS

La Table du Sauternais
T: 05 56 63 43 44 (Preignac)
This is an agreeable place to eat
in the centre of the Sauternes,
offering some surprising and
inventive dishes. Set menus start
around FF100.

Le Saprien
T: 05 56 63 60 87 (Sauternes)
The area's best restaurant outside
Langon, with a pleasant garden and
terrace. Recommended is the *soupe
de crustacés parfumée au safran*. Set
menus from about FF120 (cheaper
lunch menu).

Above *A sign advertises the
modest Maison de Sauternes.*
Top *Harvesting at Château
d'Yquem. No cost is spared here in
order to produce what is generally
regarded as the world's finest sweet
wine. The pickers are sent into the
vineyard as many times as necessary
to hand-select only those botrytised
grapes that have reached peak
ripeness. This process can continue
for several weeks.*

that causes a special form of rot in the grapes. Under the
autumn sun the mist has gone by about 11am, but by then the
fungus will have settled on the grapes, starting to affect them.

Unlike other kinds of rot, this one is exceedingly
beneficial for the fruit. That is why it is called *pourriture noble*,
or 'noble rot'. Through evaporation the affected grapes lose a
lot of their moisture, so that only juice concentrated into a
syrup is left. A certain amount of acid is also lost and the
aroma of the grapes changes. The affected fruit does not look
pleasant, becoming rather shrivelled. But appearances deceive,
for this is the basis of golden Sauternes. *Pourriture noble* can
only occur on very ripe grapes. The grower must wait until
late in the season before picking. This is taking a great risk:
the warm autumn weather quite often
breaks and rain and cold lead to a wholly
unsuccessful crop. If, however, everything
goes to plan, the grapes are picked around
the end of October. This is done with the
very greatest care: bunches with over-ripe
grapes affected by the botrytis are selected
by hand. As the degree of ripeness can
vary even within the same vineyard, the
pickers need to search the vines several
times over. Weeks are needed to carry out
what normally takes only few days. The
harvesting alone makes Sauternes much
more expensive than other wines. The yields are low, too. A
vinicultural rule of thumb is that every vine produces one
bottle of wine. At Château d'Yquem every vine gives just one
glass! The legally permitted maximum yield is 25 hectolitres
of wine per hectare; many do not even reach this low figure.

A good Sauternes is a complex wine with surprising
effects on all the senses. A beautiful, intense golden colour
is followed by a richly nuanced bouquet with impressions of
honey, nuts and apricots. The taste is improved by age: some
young Sauternes, however fresh and pure, have much less

depth and complexity than those with some maturity.

Sauternes from recent vintages are often drunk as aperitifs, or with *pâté de foie gras* (a somewhat lighter Loupiac is often preferred with duck's liver). Older, mature Sauternes can go excellently with the blue-veined Roquefort cheeses.

The region

The Sauternes district is divided into five communes: Barsac, Preignac, Bommes, Fargues, and Sauternes. The most northern is Barsac. This is distinct from all the others in that it is entitled to its own appellation, 'Barsac', as well as AC Sauternes. The Barsac landscape is fairly flat, Preignac's less so, while in Bommes, Fargues and Sauternes there are some decent hills. Barsac is the oldest wine village hereabouts: the remains of Roman villas have been found beside the church. By the main door of this church there are two marks showing how high the River Garonne rose in the floods of 1770 and 1930. Preignac is a typical main road village, with an 18th-century church (with a cupola), and a few wine-tasting rooms. Signposts show the way to Château de Malle, an

Auberge les Vignes
T: 05 56 76 60 06 (Sauternes)
Convivial restaurant by the Place de l'Eglise, serving classic regional dishes. Excellent list of regional wines.

RECOMMENDED PRODUCERS

Château Climens
Cru Classé (1er)
T: 05 56 27 15 33, F: 05 56 27 21 04
(Barsac)
Refined, rich, elegant wine.

Château Coutet
Cru Classé (1er)
T: 05 56 27 15 46, F: 05 56 27 02 20
(Barsac)
Noble, refined Barsac. In really great years a 'Cuvée Madame' is made. A lovely dry Graves is also produced.

Château Gravas
I: 05 56 27 15 20, F: 05 56 27 29 83
(Barsac)
Wine with a golden lustre and a delicous touch of *pourriture noble*.

Château Nairac
Cru Classé (2ème)
T: 05 56 27 16 16, F: 05 56 27 26 50
(Barsac)
Sauternes with style and finesse.

Château La Tour Blanche
Cru Classé (1er)
T: 05 57 98 02 70, F: 05 57 98 02 78
(Bommes)
Remarkable wine from the agricultural school here: it has a fresh aroma and a delicious concentrated taste.

Château Lafaurie-Peyraguey
Cru Classé (1er)
T: 05 56 76 60 54, F: 05 56 76 61 89
(Fargues)
Wine with style and an intense richness of bouquet and taste.

Château Rieussec
Cru Classé (1er)
T: 05 56 73 18 18, F: 05 56 59 26 83
(Fargues)
Impressive sweet wine; among the best in the area. Fine palate and concentrated finish. Notable dry white.

Château Bastor Lamontagne
T: 05 56 63 27 66, F: 05 56 76 87 03
(Preignac)
Great, luxurious; rival to *crus classés*.

Château Gillette
T: 05 56 76 28 44, F: 05 56 76 28 43
(Preignac)
Remarkable wine that matures for at least 20 years before being bottled. Very vital, with a sweet taste of caramel and honey.

Left *Château Bastor-Lamontagne in the commune of Preignac produces remarkable Sauternes, belying its cru bourgeois status.*

Château Haut-Bergeron
T: 05 56 63 24 76, F: 05 56 63 23 31
(Preignac)
Generous Sauternes; many awards.

Château de Malle
Cru Classé (2ème)
T: 05 56 63 28 67, F: 05 56 76 82 40
(Preignac)
In good years this is a complex,
intense wine. The château, a
monument, merits a visit.

Château Suduiraut
Cru Classé (1er)
T: 05 56 73 24 20, F: 05 56 73 17 28
(Preignac)
An almost decadently luxurious wine.

Château d'Arche
Cru Classé (2ème)
T: 05 56 76 66 55, F: 05 56 97 95 67
(Sauternes)
Luxurious, aromatic.

Château Guiraud
Cru Classé (1er)
T: 05 56 76 61 01, F: 05 56 76 67 52
(Sauternes)
Strikingly fresh, complex Sauternes.

Château Raymond-Lafon
T: 05 56 63 21 01, F: 05 56 63 19 58
(Sauternes)
Made in the same way as d'Yquem –
a luxurious sweet wine.

Château d'Yquem
Premier Cru Supérieur
T: 05 56 63 21 05, F: 05 57 98 07 08
(Sauternes)
Legendary, very expensive wine, the
very best Sauternes and a feast for
the senses, as is dry wine 'Y'.

Main picture *Harvesting at
Château d'Arche, one of the three
properties in Sauternes classified in
1855 as a second growth.*
Below *The Maison du Vin, in the
Place de la Mairie in Sauternes, sells
a variety of local wines.*

historic monument well worth a visit. Flanked by its pepper-pot towers, this 17th-century building has Italian gardens and a large collection of *objets d'art* and furniture, as well as some interesting fireplaces, a fine chapel and the most important collection of silhouettes in Europe. These are life-size figures carved in wood. They were used both in theatrical performances and as firescreens when hearths blazed too fiercely. Bommes is a small village, settled around a Romanesque church. Worth a visit is Château Lafaurie-Peyraguey, a castle dating in part from the 13th century.

Sauternes is especially pretty if you drive there from Bommes, approaching from a slope leading down into the village. On the wide, bare square, the Maison du Vin stocks well-known châteaux wines and a good own-brand wine.

The most impressive château in every respect here is d'Yquem, resplendent in its approachable on a 75-metre hill. With its gently sloping hills, the Sauternes district is a very pleasant area to visit. There is a well-signposted *Circuit du Sauternais* to explore and the châteaux are easy to find if you

LANGON

RESTAURANTS

Claude Darroze
T: 05 56 63 00 48, F: 05 56 63 41 15
Darroze belongs amongst the
very greatest in the Gironde. A
summertime meal on the terrace
here is a unique experience. The
modern cuisine has a classic basis.
Customers are made to feel very
welcome. Set menus from about
FF300. Nicely furnished rooms at
around FF350.

Le Brion
T: 05 56 76 27 75
Pleasant restaurant where the décor
creates the atmosphere. Modern
interpretations of regional fare. Set
menus from about FF100.

RECOMMENDED PRODUCERS

Château Brondelle
T: 05 56 62 38 14, F: 05 56 62 23 14
(Langon)
Respectable, not over-firm red Graves;
cool-tasting, fragrant and fruity white.

Château Camus
T: 05 56 63 13 29, F: 05 56 63 11 57
(St-Pierre de Mons)
Honest red Graves, agreeably fruity.

Château Respide Médeville
T: 05 56 76 28 44, F 05 56 76 28 43
(Toulenne)
Both the red and white are among
the better Graves wines: the white is
luxurious and full of character, the red
is distinguished by its fruit and wood.

Château St-Robert
T: 05 56 63 27 66, F: 05 56 76 87 03
(Pujols-sur-Ciron)
Outstanding red Graves; newish estate.

Château du Gaillat
T: 05 56 63 50 77, F: 05 56 62 20 96
(Langon)
Deep dark notes of leather, and dried
prune flavours supported by good
tannin, give this wine great breeding.

follow the signs. Driving round does not take long as this is
a small area. The Ciron Valley is particularly appealing. It is
best simply to leave the car and walk, as this is an ideal
setting for a picnic.

Langon and its environs
Langon is where the people of the Sauternes do their weekly
shopping and there is a busy Saturday market. The town is
at a meeting of the ways: Les Landes, Entre-Deux-Mers and
the motorway to Toulouse are within easy reach. The quays
along the River Garonne are lovely to walk along.

About 10 kilometres to the south, between Langon and
Bazas, is Mazères with its Château de Roquetaillade. This is
a massive, 14th-century castle. Near to it are the ruins of a
more primitive fortification, the Saint-Michel chapel with
its oriental interior, and a 13th-century dovecot.

And rather more interesting than Langon is the old
fortified town of Bazas. There is another bustling market
here, held on the square in front of the Gothic cathedral.
Cattle are chased through the streets on the Thursday before
Shrovetide – the town has given its name to good quality
beef, *boeuf de Bazas*. In this pleasant little town there is a
unique and not very well known museum of antiquities with
an *apothicairerie*, or apothecary's shop. The Saint-Antoine
hospital used to be outside the town gates and was intended
for the care of pilgrims going to Santiago de Compostela.

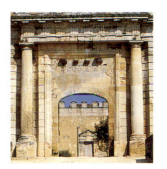

Entre-Deux-Mers

The *mers* ('seas') are in fact two tidal rivers – the Dordogne and the Garonne – the ebb and flow of which are perceptible even above Libourne. These form the two natural boundaries of Entre-Deux-Mers. The third boundary containing this wedge-shaped district is the eastern border of the Gironde *département*. Entre-Deux-Mers is the largest Bordeaux wine area, stretching for 80 kilometres southeast of the town, 30 kilometres across at its widest point.

This land of two rivers is made up of various appellations, of which Entre-Deux-Mers itself is by far the most important. Until the 1970s its semi-sweet, somewhat insipid wines were of barely any interest to wine-lovers. But quality has made great strides forward and today the name is used exclusively for sound dry whites. However, there is everything here, from strong reds and light rosés, to dry and fully sweet whites.

Entre-Deux-Mers reds remain of key importance: many Bordeaux brand names owe their existence to them. The hilly appellation of Premières Côtes de Bordeaux in the west is a nursery for an increasing number of very good wines. Also well worth discovering are the sweet wines of Cadillac. And further south along the Garonne, there are two enclaves, Loupiac and Sainte-Croix-du-Mont. These lie directly opposite Sauternes and produce comparable dessert white wines, if perhaps rather less rich, sweet or intense. Further south again comes the Bordeaux-Saint-Macaire appellation; most of its red wine is sold as Bordeaux or Bordeaux Supérieur, although now and then you will come across a white. In the extreme northeast there is the Sainte-Foy-Bordeaux area, and in the northwest, between Libourne and Bordeaux, the relatively unknown Graves de Vayres for pleasant red and dry white wines.

Left *Oyster-catching and farming is widespread in the Entre-Deux-Mers region. The oysters are delicious served with the crisp dry white wines of the area, particularly those based on Sauvignon Blanc.*

Right *Château de Tastes' lies in Sainte-Croix-du-Mont, overlooking the Garonne Valley and the Sauternes district on the other bank. The château used to make wine, but now serves the municipality dates from 1230.*

ENTRE-DEUX-MERS

HOTELS

Château de la Tour
T: 05 56 76 92 00, F: 05 56 62 11 59
(Béguey)
With a view over the nearby castle at Cadillac. Comfortable rooms from about FF575. Swimming pool, terrace, and restaurant serving classic dishes (menus from about FF150).

Le Saint-Martin
T: 05 56 67 02 67, F: 05 56 67 15 75
(Langoiran)
On the river, and therefore fairly quiet. Small, pleasant rooms in light colours; minuscule bathrooms. Prices start under FF300. Cosy restaurant with set menus from about FF100. Also ideal as a base for visiting the Graves region, only minutes away across the bridge.

Château du Parc
T: 05 56 61 69 18, F: 05 56 61 69 23
(Saint-Ferme)
This is one of the best places to stay in the Entre-Deux-Mers. It has seven tastefully decorated rooms, a garden and a swimming pool. Prices from about FF700. The château is a former residence of the abbots of the Saint-Ferme monastary.

Grand Hôtel
T: 05 57 46 00 08, F: 05 57 46 50 70
(Ste-Foy-la-Grande)
In the main street (with parking nearby). Decent rooms with high ceilings (prices from about FF300). On warm days, lunch and dinner are served on the terrace. Good regional food in generous helpings (from about FF135 for a set menu). An excellent starting point for the discovery of the charming Ste-Foy Bordeaux district.

RESTAURANTS

St-James (Bouliac)
T: 05 57 97 06 00
For years now this has been the best place to eat in the Gironde. Worth a detour for the excellent, inventive cooking of Jean-Marie Amat. Set menus from around FF300. Long, impressive wine list. St-James also owns the Hauterive hotel. The rooms here are not just contemporary but positively progressive. Prices from FF800.

Between the rivers

Entre-Deux-Mers, between the Dordogne and Garonne rivers, is an extensive area with many monasteries, abbeys, Romanesque churches, forts, castles and small fortified towns, or *bastides* – all are reminders of the wars between the French and English, which came to an end in 1453. The landscape is one of hills and valleys, offering ever-changing views out over vineyards, meadows, woods and fields.

Routes

From Bordeaux there are a number of possible sight-seeing routes. The choice will depend on your interests and time available. As a guideline, a complete circular tour will take at least a day. One possible route is Bordeaux, Floirac, Latresne, Créon, Cadillac, La Réole, Monségur, Sauveterre-de-Guyenne, Castelviel, Rauzan, Branne, then Bordeaux.

In Quinsac at the Maison du Vin for the Premières Côtes de Bordeaux there is a detailed route map available (*Balades*

Le Bistroy
T: 05 57 97 06 06 (Bouliac)
A simpler edition of the St-James, but with equally tasty cooking. Set menus start below FF200. To be avoided on hot, sunny days as the tables are set in the conservatory.

Hôtel de France
T: 05 56 84 50 06 (Branne)
On the market square, and a good place to eat. Classic cuisine with regional dishes such as *sole aux cèpes* and *profiterols au chocolat*. Set menus from around FF100. Rooms about FF300.

Les Fontaines
T: 05 56 61 15 25 (La Réole)
Sympathetic restaurant with a savoury cuisine; try the *matelote de poissons*. Menus from about FF100.

Château Camiac
T: 05 56 23 20 85, F: 05 56 23 38 84 (Créon)
Excellent *hostellerie* where the cooking is impressive (try the pigeon dishes) and the rooms are comfortable – menus from about FF175, rooms from FF450 to around FF1,300. On the road to Branne

La Fontine
T: 05 56 61 11 81 (Fontet)
Popular restaurant serving regional dishes, such as *magret grillé escaloppé de foie gras*. Set menus from FF75.

Les Remparts
T: 05 56 47 43 46 (Gensac)
Here, with a lovely view of the valley, you can enjoy the food in one of the up-and-coming restaurants of the Ste-Foy Bordeaux region. Menus from about FF150. Six simple rooms.

Les Trois Cèdres
T: 05 56 71 10 70 (Gironde-sur-Dropt)
From the outside you would not think there was a young master-chef in the kitchen. Surprising cuisine – for example, *blignis de guanaja et caviar de pommes au nougat*. Set menus start around FF120. There are a few rooms here at about FF300 (always ask for one at the back).

Le Belvédere
T: 05 57 47 40 33 (Juillac)
Perched on a high hill near the Dordogne. Apart from the splendid view, you can enjoy regional specialities here, such as sturgeon and *confit de canard*. Set menus from about FF100. Follow the signs from the village.

Le Coq Sauvage
T: 05 56 20 41 04 (St-Loubes)
By the little harbour on the Dordogne stands this congenial restaurant, with an attractive indoor garden. Classic, appetising regional dishes; set menus from about FF150. Six rooms available, around FF300.

en Premières Côtes de Bordeaux) for this appellation. And the modern Maison des Bordeaux at Beychac–et–Cailleau, set up by the combined Bordeaux Supérieur producers, serves as an information centre for visits to wine estates. There is also a well-stocked *vinothèque* in the basement.

Useful route descriptions are also available at the Office du Tourisme in Bordeaux. These relate to themes other than wine: *circuit des églises fortifiées*, *circuit des villes fortifiées*, *circuit des souterrains* and of course *les bastides de la Gironde*. All the routes cover distances of 140 to 200 kilometres. What follows below are the sights to see, the restaurants, and the wine producers in the most important of the small towns and villages of the area. To help the reader they have been put in alphabetical order.

Baurech dates back to the Verego Roman villa, residence of Leontius II and a large wine estate of the time. In **Béguey** a splendid panorama of the surrounding country can be seen from the highest point in the hills. Architectural high points

Au Vieux Logis
T: 05 56 78 92 99 (St-Loubes)
This well-known restaurant with its good cooking is five minutes from the golf course. Set menus start at around FF120. Within 150 metres there is a small hotel with simple, clean rooms (ask for one at the back). Prices from about FF275.

L'Abricotier
T: 05 56 76 83 63 (St-Macaire)
The décor in this restaurant is contemporary, as is the chef's culinary skill: creativity is the mark of his cuisine. Ample set menus, from about FF130.

RECOMMENDED PRODUCERS

Château Carignan
T: 05 56 21 21 30, F: 05 56 78 36 65 (Carignan)
Generous red Premières Côtes de Bordeaux, and an impressive château.

Château Carsin
T: 05 56 76 93 06, F: 05 56 62 64 80 (Rions)
Produces delicious red and white wines. The proprietor is Finnish.

Château Reynon
T: 05 56 62 96 51, F: 05 56 62 14 84 (Béguey)
Outstanding dry white wine, with subtle aromas, and elegant yet juicy fruit. The red (a Premières Côtes de Bordeaux) is deep-coloured, powerful, with fruit, vanilla and good length.

Château Lesparre
T: 05 57 24 51 23, F: 05 57 24 03 99 (Beychac-et-Cailleau)
Large range of very good wines, including red Graves de Vayres.

Château Fayau
T: 05 56 62 65 80 (Cadillac)
Good red Bordeaux Supérieur with intense aroma and long length. The sweet white has often won awards.

Château de Haux
T: 05 56 23 35 07, F: 05 56 23 25 29 (Haux)
Delicious red Premières Côtes de Bordeaux that undergoes barrel ageing. The Danish, owners have several other wine estates too.

Château Langoiran
T: 05 56 67 08 55, F: 05 56 67 32 87 (Langoiran)
Underground cellars of the ruins of the Langoiran castle, perched on a hill above the village. The best red Premières Côtes de Bordeaux is called Château Tour de Langoiran.

Château Suau
T: 05 56 72 19 06, F: 05 56 72 12 43
Totally renovated property, a former hunting lodge, where attractive red and white wines are produced.

are the remains of a Roman harbour wall and the 18th-century Peyran estate. In **Beychac-et-Cailleau** there are two attractions: an excellent golf course and the Maison des Bordeaux et Bordeaux Supérieur – the embassy for producers.

Blasimon's Benedictine abbey (largely in ruins) has a marvellous main door with allegorical representations of the virtues and vices surrounding it. A small collection of archaeological finds is displayed in the *mairie*. **Bouliac**, is set quite high up, and is best known for its restaurants. It has a 12th-century church well worth seeing, too, built on the foundations of the Roman villa Vodol (Vodollacum Bodollacum became Bouliac), and a noted place of refuge during the Hundred Years War. **Branne** is a small harbour on the Dordogne near Libourne, at its most beautiful in the light of the setting sun. Its neo-Gothic church is 19th-century.

Cadillac has its own appellation – for sweet whites (Cadillac red wine is sold as Bordeaux or Bordeaux Supérieur). The town itself, founded in the 13th century, is still partly walled. In the centre there stands an imposing castle of the ducs d'Epernon – now home to the Maison du Vin. This stronghold was built in the 17th century, and its past functions have included a spell as a women's prison. Inside are rooms with great fireplaces and beautifully painted ceilings. An important market is held in the town every Saturday.

In **Cambes**, the interior of the Romanesque church of Saint-Martin has been classified as a historic monument. Also worth seeing here is the Château du Peyrat, built in 1655. And at **Camblanes et Meynac** around the church there is a pleasant terrace, and a Roman mosaic in the *mairie*. **Capian** is well worth a visit to see its old mill foundations (many excavations have been carried out), the medieval tower used by the Télégraphe de Chappe, and the Romanesque church of Saint-Saturnin, where a Roman wine cask is preserved. Attractive sight-seeing routes are set out.

For centuries now **Carignan de Bordeaux** has been an area where well-to-do Bordeaux citizens have relaxed in environs steeped in history. The castles of Carignan (parts of it 15th century) and Canteloup (also a well-known wine estate), make fascinating visits, as does the 12th-century church. Then in **Castelviel** the local church, sited on a hill, has a beautiful porch; one of the reliefs shows a vine being pruned.

Cénac, an important stopping place for pilgrims en route to Santiago de Compostela, lies in particularly beautiful surroundings, with much to explore. A splendid view across the River Garonne can be enjoyed between Cénac and Montillac. And near **Créon** stands the most famous abbey of

Château Brethous
T: 05 56 20 77 75
(Camblanes-et-Meynac)
One of the oldest wine estates in Camblanes. Firm, supple red wine.
Château du Grand Moueys
T: 05 57 97 04 44, F: 05 57 97 04 60
(Capian)
German-owned, curious-looking neo-Gothic castle where the red Premières Côtes de Bordeaux and the barrel-fermented white Bordeaux deserve attention.

Left *The Château de Cadillac, a 12th-century fortress, which dominates the small wine town Cadillac.* Below *The Premières Côtes de Bordeaux. Some semi-sweet white wines are made, but the Merlot-based reds deserve most attention.*

Above *The dramatic remains of a 13th-century fortress and keep at Langoiran, in the southern part of the Premières Côtes de Bordeaux.*

Château Barreyre
T: 05 56 67 02 03, F: 05 56 67 59 07
(Langoiran)
The *chai* where the Cuvée Spéciale matures, a red Premières Côtes de Bordeaux, is one of the most beautiful in the region; modern art is regularly on display here.

Château Roques Mauriac
T: 05 57 40 51 84, F: 05 57 40 55 48
(Doulezon)
The Hélène *cuvée* is one of the great stars in Entre-Deux-Mers. This Bordeaux Supérieur is matured in wood and is packed with fruit.

Château Bonnet
T: 05 57 25 58 58, F: 05 57 74 98 59
(Grézillac)
Juicy, mouth-filling white with appealing aromas of fruit and spring flowers. Fruity, supple red is also pleasing.

Entre-Deux-Mers, La Sauve Majeure. Its tower dates from 1230 and is still in good, climbable condition: the view from the top is most impressive. The abbey itself (dating from 1079) is rather dilapidated but fascinating. There is also a museum.

Espiet exemplifies the fact that besides the *bastides* and fortified churches in Entre-Deux-Mers there are also fortified mills: Moulin Neuf here is one of the most elegant. So is the fountain of Saint-Aignan: its water was said to cure eye troubles and leprosy. **Gabarnac**'s 12th-century Romanesque church is a gem – especially for its main door, a classified historic monument. There are also two old 18th-century mills in the village. Visiting the mill in **Gornac** is also recommended (by appointment). Inside is a country life museum.

Haux is a 16th-century château, rebuilt as a fortress in the 17th century, surviving now as a wine estate. Wines from past vintages can be bought here. In **Langoiran** the Château de Langoiran is now little more than a ruin, but in the old stone quarries (*carrières*) excellent wines are matured. There is also a 12th-century church, a botanical park (the Parc de Peyruche) and a zoo. **Lestiac**, close to Château de Langoiran, is a traditional fishing spot, and a notable location for catching *aloses* (shad). And **Loubes** has one of the finest fortified mills in Entre-Deux-Mers, with entrance ways on two storeys. It was built this way to cope when the floods came.

Loupiac has a growing reputation in France. Its wines are white, full-flavoured and almost liqueur-like – very like Sainte-Croix-du-Mont. Locally they are drunk young as aperitifs, and taste excellent with *foie de canard*. Older wines deliciously complement fruit tarts. An archaeological dig in Loupiac has exposed a Roman bath complete with mosaics. Its church has been declared a monument and is also worth a visit.

The charming village of **Quinsac** houses the Maison du Vin for the Premières Côtes de Bordeaux. It has an engaging fountain set into the wall of the presbytery, the *fontaine du Clairet*. There is a market on Wednesdays. Above the village of **Rauzan**, are the ruins of Château de Duras (12–15th century). One of the largest and best of France's cooperatives is here, too, the Union des Producteurs de Rauzan.

Close to the little town of **La Réole** the abbey of Saint-Ferme still survives. It was built by Cluniac monks and partly rebuilt after 1585 – today it serves as a town hall. The monumental fireplace in its west wing is particularly striking. Thursday is La Réole's market day. Medieval **Rions** is known as 'Carcassonne of the Gironde', and there is some similarity to the famous fortified town. Its surrounding 14th-century walls are not the only architectural high points: others are the Tour du Lhyan, the citadel, the Charles VII cave, and the 12th-century church. the church at **Saint-André-du-Bois** has little history to recount, but the impressive cedars that stand around it could tell some tales. The village is most famous as home to artist Toulouse-Lautrec, who lived in the Château de Malromé – reproductions of his paintings hang in the château. A few *chambres d'hôte* are available. Then, well worth seeing at **Saint-Caprais de Bordeaux**, is the 11th- and 12th-century church. A Virgin and Child here are among some of the top examples of French medieval sculpture.

Sainte-Croix-du-Mont is well known for its sweet white wines, sometimes reaching the richness of Sauternes. The

Château du Bru
T: 05 57 46 12 71, F: 05 57 46 10 64
(St-Avit-St-Nazaire)
Offers a portfolio of remarkable wines, like an oak-matured white Ste-Foy-Bordeaux and a mouth-filling red Cuvée Réservée (Bordeaux Supérieur).

Château de Seguin
T: 05 56 21 97 84, F: 05 57 78 34 85
(Lignan)
A Bordeaux Supérieur that regularly wins medals. Harmonious wine, supple and long in its finish. Deserves a few years' patience.

Clos Jean
T: 05 56 62 99 83, F: 05 56 62 93 55
(Loupiac)
Dry white – from a village known for its sweet wine. A rich aroma and a deep, complex taste characterise this wine. The Loupiac is also good.

Château Roquefort
T: 05 56 23 97 48, F: 05 56 23 51 44
(Lugasson)
White wine (Cuvée Spéciale) matured in wood, with a flowery, complex taste.

Domaine de Chastelet
T: 05 56 72 61 96, F: 05 56 72 45 63
(Quinsac)
Deep-coloured Premières Côtes de Bordeaux with oak on the nose and the palate.

Château Moulin de Launay
T: 05 56 61 31 51, F: 05 56 61 40 22
(Soussac)
One of the sure-value Entre-Deux-Mers.

Château Hostens-Picant
T: 05 57 46 38 11, F: 05 57 46 26 23
(Clos Lèves-et-Thoumeyragues)
The dry white Cuvée des Demoiselles is fermented in new barrels and has the class of a good Graves or Pessac-Léognan, while the red wine (also a Ste-Foy Bordeaux) merits discovering too.

Château Loubens
T: 05 56 62 01 25, F: 05 56 76 71 65
(Ste-Croix-du-Mont)
One of the stars of its appellation.

Château Lousteau-Vieil
T: 05 56 62 01 15, F: 05 56 62 01 68
(Ste-Croix-du-Mont)
Wonderful sweet wine that can be compared to a Barsac.

Left Loupiac produces sweet white wines that are rich and liqueur-like and, along with those of Ste-Croix-du-Mont, offer good value alternatives to Sauternes and Barsac.

locals drink them as aperitifs, and with poultry, white meat and game. There is a tasting cellar in one of the local *caves* where you can sample them. From the church square there is a splendid view out over the valley of the Garonne, Sauternes and the Graves district. The village is also renowned for its fossil oyster beds and Château de Tastes, a castle dating from the 14th and 15th centuries.

Sainte-Foy-la-Grande is a little hamlet steeped in history. As you walk through there are a number of ancient buildings and crumbling old fortifications. And in **Saint-Germain-du-Puch**, a simple wine village hiding more clues to the past than you'd expect, there are Roman mosaics in the church and a model of 14th-century military architecture in the Château du Grand Puch.

Medieval **Saint-Macaire**, built on a cliff, gives its name to the Côtes de Bordeaux Saint-Macaire appellation. Good to see are the merchants' houses, the intricate arcading on the square, the defensive walls, and the church. Also there is the Aquitaine postal museum and a museum of tropical fish.

Château La Rame
T: 05 56 62 01 50, F: 05 56 62 01 94
(Ste-Croix-du-Mont)
Unctuous wine for keeping.
Château Jonqueyres
(St-Germain-du-Puch)
Intense red wine with smooth, supple tannin and packed with fruit.
Château de Malagar
T: 05 56 95 53 00, F: 05 56 59 39 89
(St-Maixant)
Elegant, attractive red wine and two decent white ones. The château is also a museum: Nobel Prize winner François Mauriac, the great writer, lived and worked here.
Château Le Grand Verdus
T: 05 56 30 64 22, F: 05 56 23 71 37
(Sadirac)
Splendid, perfectly structured red Cuvée Réservée (Bordeaux Supérieur) with delicious hints of oak.
Château la Clyde
T: 05 56 67 56 84, F: 05 56 67 12 06
(Tabanac)
One of the better red wines from the Premières Côtes de Bordeaux: generous, firm and supple.
Château de Plassane
T: 05 56 67 53 16, F: 05 56 67 26 28
(Tabanac)
At the end of the Revolution, the Clauzel family rebuilt the château in a Palladian style. Substantial red wine with allure.

The French author François Mauriac often spent time at Château de Malagar in **Saint-Maixant**. Mauriac was involved in trying out the various pathways (on horseback, bicycle or foot) now marked around the village. The château functions as a museum and a wine estate. **Sauveterre-de-Guyenne** is an attractive *bastide* with four of its original gateways. At the Bassellerie bakery here you can buy excellent *pain à l'ancienne* – traditional bread. Then in **Soulignac** the focal point is a windmill – the only one in Entre-Deux-Mers built to produce electricity. The village of **Targon** is best known for its Romanesque-style church. And the great attraction of **Vayres** is the castle, once the property of Henry IV of France, and now used as a conference centre. It has a fine terrace with a very large flight of steps and a garden that leads down to the Gironde. Also impressive is the *pigeonnier*, potentially home to some 2,600 birds. Vayres is the centre of the small wine district of Graves de Vayre, making supple red and white wines. The latter used to be semi-sweet, but fortunately are now following the trend towards dry wines.

Finally **Verdelais**, which has a notable basilica, built over eight centuries: Romanesque, Gothic and Baroque in style. Henri de Toulouse-Lautrec lies buried in the cemetery here.

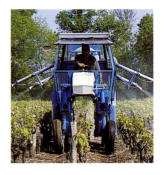

Far left and main picture *The monumental Château de Vayres which attracts many visitors.* Above *Spraying protects vines from insects and fungal diseases.*

Château Toutigeac
T: 05 56 23 90 10, F: 05 56 23 67 21 (Targon)
For his white wine the owner uses the Entre-Deux-Mers Haut Benauge appellation. The wine is lively and fresh. Toutigeac's red Bordeaux is meant to be drunk young; better than average quality.

SPECIAL INTEREST

An artist works in the hamlet of Morizès, near to La Réole (*Tel: 05 56 71 45 56*); her speciality is handmade roof tiles fired in a Gallo-Roman oven.

On November 25th the fountain at Camblanes-et-Meynac spouts free wine, as does the one at Quinsac.

In Vayres, a craftsman cooper – a *tonnelier* – is still at work; he can be visited by appointment. (*Tel: 05 56 74 85 29.*)

The Libournais

On the right bank of the Dordogne lie two of the most renowned wine districts on earth: Saint-Emilion and Pomerol. Strangely enough, however, it was well into the 20th century before wines from these areas had any reputation at all; in France they were known, but few people abroad had ever heard of them. When the classification of the best Bordeaux wines was drawn up in 1855, the products of this area, the Libournais (centred on the town of Libourne), were not even considered – a fact scarcely imaginable today.

The Saint-Emilion district is bounded at the north by the little River Barbanne, to the east by the hills around Castillon-la-Bataille, on the southeast and south (from Castillon-la-Bataille to Libourne) by the Dordogne plain, and to the west by another flat, though slightly less low-lying, area extending as far as Libourne. Remarkably, these boundaries are practically identical to those laid down in 1289, when Edward I of England first drew up the Saint-Emilion area. A glance at any contour map makes the undulating countryside more than clear: the height differences range from almost 100 metres near the church in the centre to only 10 metres above sea level in the little village of Viognet.

Pomerol is a small appellation, created relatively recently in 1936. It is one of the few quality districts in Bordeaux where an official hierarchy of *crus* has never been established. But this does not alter the fact that alongside the celebrated Château Pétrus there are various other wines here that enjoy worldwide acclaim. Demand for Pomerol is greater than the supply. Prices are therefore on the expensive side.

Increasingly now, too, the district of Fronsac is mentioned in the same breath as Saint-Emilion and Pomerol. It is producing wines of increasing excellence.

Left Château St-Georges in St-Emilion-St-Georges. This historic château was built in 1774 by Victor Louis, who also built the Grand Théâtre in Bordeaux.

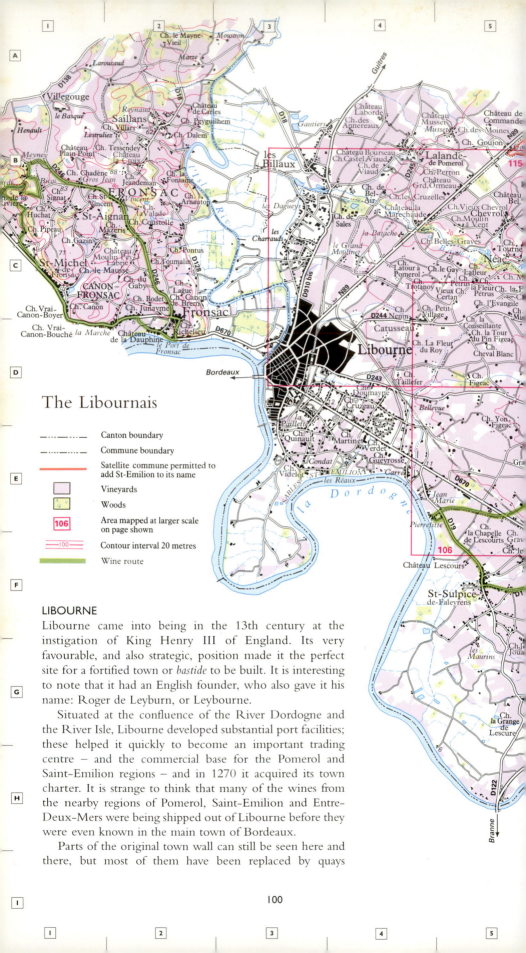

The Libournais

- – · – · – Canton boundary
- – ·· – ·· – Commune boundary
- ━━━━ Satellite commune permitted to add St-Emilion to its name
- ▨ Vineyards
- ▨ Woods
- 106 Area mapped at larger scale on page shown
- ══100══ Contour interval 20 metres
- ▬▬▬ Wine route

LIBOURNE

Libourne came into being in the 13th century at the instigation of King Henry III of England. Its very favourable, and also strategic, position made it the perfect site for a fortified town or *bastide* to be built. It is interesting to note that it had an English founder, who also gave it his name: Roger de Leyburn, or Leybourne.

Situated at the confluence of the River Dordogne and the River Isle, Libourne developed substantial port facilities; these helped it quickly to become an important trading centre – and the commercial base for the Pomerol and Saint-Emilion regions – and in 1270 it acquired its town charter. It is strange to think that many of the wines from the nearby regions of Pomerol, Saint-Emilion and Entre-Deux-Mers were being shipped out of Libourne before they were even known in the main town of Bordeaux.

Parts of the original town wall can still be seen here and there, but most of them have been replaced by quays

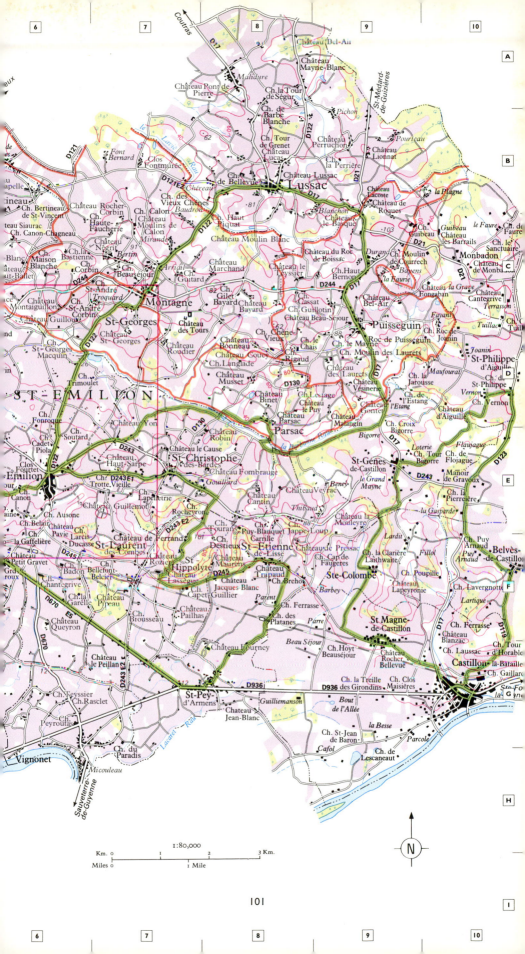

LIBOURNE

🗝 HOTELS

Le Duc de Libourne
9 Rue des Treilles
T: 05 57 74 04 47, F: 05 57 25 08 19
Simple hotel, close to the station.
Rooms from about FF230.
Decazes
22 Place Decazes
T: 05 57 25 18 70, F: 05 57 25 19 59
Also has a bar and brasserie. Rooms
of rural simplicity. From FF250.

🍽 RESTAURANTS

LIBOURNE
Chez Servais
14 Place Descazes
Tel: 05 57 51 83 97
Extensive wine list and fish as a
speciality. Quality restaurant; set
menus from around FF130.

*Below and far right There is a
thrice-weekly market in the main
square of Libourne selling many
local delicacies. Cafés are also
plentiful in the centre.*

bordered by plane trees. It is the confluence of the two
rivers that gives Libourne its particular character, however,
and parts of the original town, including the Tour de Grand
Port, are to be found near this salient feature.

Libourne deserves to be toured on foot. Motorists who
drive quickly through are greatly mistaken in doing so. The
beautifully restored Carmelite chapel alone, which now
serves as an exhibition centre, more than justifies a stop to
look round. The Rue des Murs, Rue du Port-Coiffe, and
Rue des Chais date back to Libourne's 13th-century origins.
So does Rue Carreyron: a medieval street and another of
the main places of interest – also well worth a visit. In the
Place Abel Surchamp stands the 15th-
century town hall, restored in the early
1900s. It houses a number of interesting
items, including the Livre Velu, a calf-
bound book containing the various
enactments of the town and its district,
drawn up by the kings of England
between the 13th and 15th centuries. In
the same square is the Musée des Beaux-
Arts with a fine collection of paintings to
peruse – including works from the
Flemish and Italian schools of the 16th
century. The square itself is surrounded

Left *The ancient town of Libourne;*
the vineyards of Pomerol fan out
from here.

Chanzy Le Bistrot
16 Rue Chanzy
T: 05 57 51 84 26
Modest bistro with reasonable food.
Set menus start from around FF100,
and affordable wines.

SABLON-DE-GUITRES
Auberge de l'Isle
T: 05 57 69 22 58
Good cuisine here, with classic dishes
of the region. There are seven simple
rooms below the FF200 mark.

by houses and arcades. A bustling market is held there
three days a week. Some of Libourne's most important
wine businesses are situated on the Quai Prieurat
overlooking the Dordogne. This wine trade quay, which
could be compared to the Quai des Chartrons in Bordeaux,
has kept much of its original character. The *chais*, covering
an area of some hectares, extend far back behind the
simple frontages. The words '*Les Amis du Vin*' appear on
some of them, indicating a mail–order business that also has
a shop on the quay.

SAINT-EMILION

HOTELS

Château Grand Barrail
T: 05 57 55 37 00, F: 05 57 55 37 49
Beautifully restored after 30 years of
neglect. Extremely comfortable rooms
in the castle itself as well as a new
wing) for around FF950. Set dinner
from FF200; lunch is cheaper. Mainly
classic dishes. Wonderful place to stay.

Hostellerie de Plaisance
T: 05 57 55 07 55, F: 05 57 74 41 11
Comfortable, and unique in its central
position. All rooms are named after a
château, and some have spectacular

bathrooms. Prices from around FF500.
Cooking sometimes varies. Impressive
wine list with the region's good names.

Logis des Remparts
T: 05 57 24 70 43, F: 05 57 74 47 44
Good hotel in centre; 15 comfortable
rooms. Prices from FF375.

Bonsai
T: 05 57 25 25 07, F: 05 57 25 26 59
Modern hotel on the road from
Libourne to Castilllon-la-Bataille:
quiet and comfortable. Rooms
from FF275.

Palais Cardinal
T: 05 57 24 72 39, F: 05 57 74 47 54
Pleasant hotel/restaurant in the
medium range. Rooms from FF350.

Above, right and far right Scenes
from Libourne, a large town of
25,000 inhabitants, founded in the
13th-century by the Englishman,
Roger de Leyburn, after whom the
town was named.

Dealing in wine actually started considerably later in
Libourne than in Bordeaux. One of the reasons for this was
the distance from Libourne down to the River Gironde,
which corresponded to one whole tide. A sailing ship
therefore needed three tides to get from the river mouth at
the Atlantic up to Libourne – in practice, two days. The
spirit of commercial enterprise seems to have eventually
arrived with settlers from the poorer Corrèze *département* at
the beginning of the 20th century. Families such as Moueix
and Janoueix settling at this time still remain today.
According to official statistics there are now more than 250
wine businesses in Libourne, but this figure does seem rather
on the high side.

As for viticulture, there are in fact hardly any vines left in
or around Libourne itself. The expansion of the town has
taken its toll and many of the vineyards have disappeared to
make way for new houses and businesses. A few still exist in
the outskirts, however; thus about 160 hectares of the Saint-
Emilion appellation are on Libourne territory, and AC
Pomerol, too, includes vineyards within the municipal
boundaries. In addition, Libourne makes a good base for
exploring the Fronsac wine district, which begins
immediately across the bridge near the Tour du Grand Pont.
From there the D670 leads to more wine regions waiting to
be explored: Saint-André-de-Cubzac, Bourg and Blaye (*see*
pages 127–135).

It is amazing that a town like Libourne should be so short of really good restaurants. Saint-Emilion is much better provided for and if you are staying in Libourne, it is worthwhile driving there for a good meal. Another possibility is to be found in the little village of Sablon-de-Guîtres. To get there, take the D910 Angoulême road and when nearly at Coutras, turn left for Guîtres. The distance is only 20 kilometres and, once you get there, you can dine right royally on the banks of the Isle at the Auberge de l'Isle.

RESTAURANTS

Francis Goullée
T: 05 57 24 70 49
Outstanding cuisine in a pleasant restaurant. Classic dishes interpreted in a modern way. Set menus from FF120 and a good, conveniently arranged wine list. Proprietor Goullée often cooks at the châteaux.

Le Tertre
T: 05 57 74 46 33
Restaurant close to the church; try the *Coq au Vin de St-Emilion*. Menus from about FF140.

L'Envers du Décor
T: 05 57 74 46 31
A real, classic *bistrot à vins*, or wine bar. Many wines sold by the glass, from other districts and other parts of the world as well. Classic cuisine attuned to wine. Service on the terrace on warm days. Set menus from about FF100.

SPECIAL INTEREST

From April to the end of September a little train runs through the streets of St-Emilion and the surrounding vineyards. The departure point is the collegiate church on the northwest side of the town, not far from the Place du Marché. The ride lasts for half an hour.

The *macarons* from the *pâtissier* Blanchez are regarded as the best. You will find the shop in the Rue Guadet, next to the post office.

In the summer months, information about wine can usually also be obtained at the Pavillon d'Accueil at St-Etienne-de-Lisse, and the Pavillon du Vin at St-Pey-d'Armens.

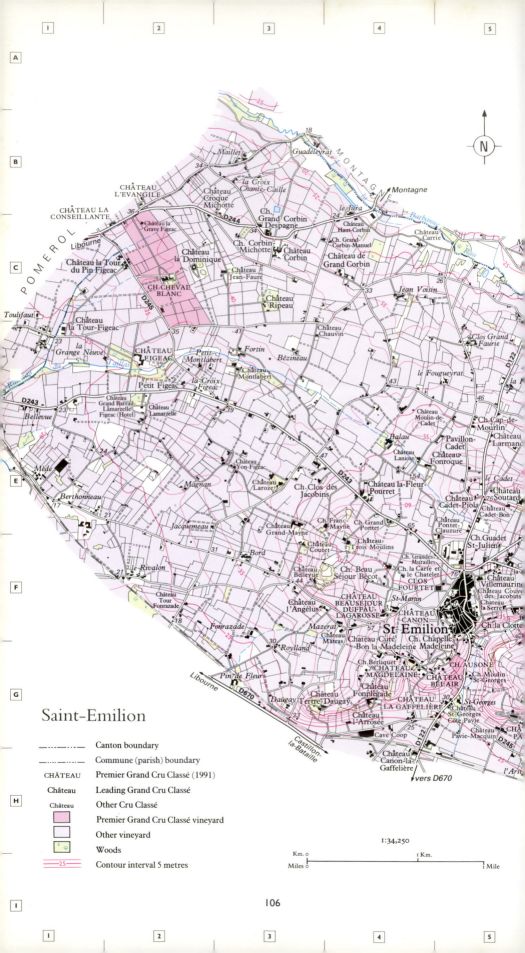

Right The beautiful, tiered hillside town of St-Emilion attracts thousands of visitors every year.

SAINT-EMILION
The town

Medieval Saint-Emilion is one of the most romantic and photogenic wine communities in the world. It lies on the slopes and top of a limestone plateau where building stone for churches, monasteries, fortifications and dwellings was once quarried. The result is a network of passages and chambers in the rock, both under the town and extending right out under the surrounding vineyards. In some cases it is even possible to walk along an underground passage from one château to another. Some of the rock chambers are so huge that banquets can be held in them for hundreds of people – this happens at Château Villemaurine on the edge of the town. Naturally enough many of these caves and passageways have been used for generations now for storing wine. A striking feature of some of them is the vine roots – including some of Saint-Emilion's best – appearing in their ceilings, poking through from the vineyards up on the limestone above.

In times of war the quarries have served as hiding places. In 1793 the tiny town was a place of refuge for a number of Bordeaux deputies pursued by republican extremists. One of these refugees was Marguerite-Elie Guadet, who was tracked down and executed. Her name appears in the Rue Guadet (the main street) and in Château Guadet-Saint-Julien.

Once again, it was the Romans who started winegrowing here. Traces of what were probably Roman vineyards can still be seen at the châteaux of Bellevue and Soutard. Also, the poet and consul Ausonius had one of his three villas in the neighbourhood – possibly where Château Ausone stands today.

Above *Looking down across the rooftops of St-Emilion.*
Below right and far right *St-Emilion has an excellent selection of bars and restaurants.*

SAINT-EMILION (continued)

RECOMMENDED PRODUCERS

Château Angélus
Premier Grand Cru Classé (B)
T: 05 57 24 71 39, F: 05 57 24 68 56
Full, rich St-Emilion with much depth, luscious fruit and smoky wood. Imposing barrel cellar.

Château l'Arrosée
Grand Cru Classé
T: 05 57 24 70 47
Distinguished wine with deep colour and a fine, generous taste: vineyards on southwest slope of the plateau.

Château Ausone
Premier Grand Cru Classé (A)
T: 05 57 24 70 26, F: 05 57 24 67 11
Showplace of the Côtes and one of only two Premiers Grands Crus Classés 'A'. The estate, named after Roman consul and poet, Ausonius, is on the edge of St-Emilion's limestone plateau, commanding long vineyard and Dordogne Valley views. Its penetratingly perfumed wines can rival great Médocs in style and finesse.

The name of the town itself comes from Saint Aemilianus (Emilion), who in the 8th century broke his pilgrim's journey to Santiago de Compostela here, and did not leave. He began to live as a hermit, gathering followers around him. The cave he inhabited is still there and can be visited. Later the Franciscans and Dominicans founded monasteries near the site, and Saint-Emilion was administered jointly by an ecclesiastical chapter and a secular body, the Jurade. In 1289 Edward I of England confirmed Saint-Emilion's status and also defined the area of its jurisdiction. This largely corresponds with the later boundaries of the wine district.

During the Hundred Years War (finally decided in favour of the French, in 1453) Saint-Emilion suffered great damage. A monastery church was almost totally destroyed. All that is left today from this time is a solitary high wall on the northwest side of the town, the Grandes Murailles monument.

The Jurade is still active, although exclusively now in the field of wine. Since being re-established in 1948 it has been engaged in representing and promoting the interests of the local vignerons. Two of the most important events in which the Jurade is involved are the judging of the new wines in June, and the declaration of the grape harvest, the *ban des vendanges*, in September. At this time the members walk through the old streets in their scarlet robes, making a colourful, photo-worthy spectacle.

The whole of Saint-Emilion has been declared a historic monument and use of motor vehicles by non-residents is banned in practically all the streets. Large car parks have therefore been laid out on the edge of the town, outside its former walls. There is so much to see in Saint-Emilion that an hour or two should certainly be set aside for a walk around. It may be a good idea to start by collecting the literature in the Office du Tourisme, which organises guided tours. Round the corner from this office is the Maison du Vin. All possible information on the wine can be obtained here, as well as details on visiting the châteaux. Anyone who is deeply interested in the Saint-Emilion wines can attend lectures in the Maison du Vin in the months of July, August and September. It costs around FF100 to do this, and there are sessions twice a day. Those taking part are let into the vinous secrets of the area in a manner that is both instructive and generous. Longer periods of instruction are also possible, an arrangement sometimes combined with meals. The Rue Guadet is where the Syndicat Viticole is established, which looks after the interests of the wine district and its producers.

The tour

A good place to begin your walk around Saint-Emilion is the Place du Clocher, opposite the Office du Tourisme. Adjoining this square is another smaller one, the Place du Marché, with a terrace often packed with colourful sunshades. The Hostellerie de Plaisance, a renowned hotel and restaurant, is in the place du Clocher. It has a wonderful terrace with fabulous views out over the town. The square takes its name from a clock tower 67 metres high. The lowest part of it is 12th-century in origin and is Romanesque; the centre part was built in Gothic style in the 14th century, and the steeple dates from the 15th century. As you wander towards the Place du Marché, you can be easily distracted by the narrow side streets, which reveal a number of wine shops full of tempting bottles. You will also find pastry cooks in Saint-Emilion who make the local *macarons*. These little almond cakes are

Château Balestard-la-Tonnelle
Grand Cru Classé
T: 05 57 74 62 06, F: 05 57 74 59 34
A very old estate – a verse from the 15th-century poet, François Villan, reproduced on the label, refers to 'the divine nectar... of Balestard'. An old stone tower on the estate has been restored and is used for receptions. A big, and at the same time vital, wine, consistent in its soundness.

Château Beauséjour
Premier Grand Cru Classé (B)
T: 05 57 24 71 61, F: 05 57 74 48 40
Pretty property on west-facing

Côtes. Traditionally made, concentrated wine with a lot of tannin and refinement: demands patience; for laying down.

Château Beau-Séjour Bécot
Premier Grand Cru Classé (B)
T: 05 57 74 46 87, F: 05 57 24 66 88
The château stands high on the plateau of St-Emilion, with fine cellars cut into the limestone. Its wine is a distinguished combination of concentration and complexity.

Château Belair
Premier Grand Cru Classé (B)
T: 05 57 24 70 94, F: 05 57 24 67 11
Close to Château Ausone and owned by Madame Heylett Dubois-Challon, co-owner of Ausone. The wine is among the best of the Côtes, with a beautiful aroma of oak and silkiness.

Château Berliquet
Grand Cru Classé
T: 05 57 24 70 71, F: 05 57 24 65 18
A substantial house in a pleasant garden, producing a harmonious wine with lots of class.

Château Canon
Premier Grand Cru Classé (B)
T: 05 57 24 70 79, F: 05 57 24 68 00
Classic St-Emilion of majestic quality from a partly walled vineyard on the limestone plateau. It is made in the traditional way for long cellaring.

Château Canon-la-Gaffelière
Grand Cru Classé
T: 05 57 24 71 33, F: 05 57 24 67 95
Deep-coloured wine with lots of fruit
and a harmonious, complex taste. It
shows charm when young, but also
has the backbone for ageing.

Château Cheval Blanc
Premier Grand Cru Classé (A)
T: 05 57 55 55 55, F: 05 57 55 55 50
The vineyard of this charming château
is close to the Pomerol boundary and
has a lot of gravel in its soil. The wine
has opulence and refinement, strength
and subtlety. Great vintages are
legendary – unsurpassed even among
the first growths of the Médoc.

Château Clos des Jacobins
Grand Cru Classé
T: 05 57 24 70 14, F: 05 57 24 68 08
Relatively supple and firm wine.

Château La Clotte
Grand Cru Classé
Tel: 05 57 24 66 85
Delicious wine with fruit and oak in
its bouquet and taste.

Château Corbin-Michotte
Grand Cru Classé
T: 05 57 51 64 88, F: 05 57 51 56 30
Harmonious, reasonably firm wine
provided with a finish rich in tannin.

Château Curé Bon
Grand Cru Classé
T: 05 57 74 43 20, F: 05 57 24 66 41
Sometimes sumptuous in taste.

Château La Dominique
Grand Cru Classé
T: 05 57 51 31 36, F: 05 57 51 63 04
This is a beautiful wine: generous and
rounded.

Château Figeac
Premier Grand Cru Classé (B)
T: 05 57 24 72 26, F: 05 57 74 45 74
Dignified château with a long history;
the estate once included what is now
Cheval Blanc and other properties.
The vineyard on low gravel hills is
70 per cent Cabernet (half Sauvignon,
the highest proportion for St-Emilion)
and the wine has a velvety softness
and great allure. It can be drunk early
but is capable of long maturing.

Château Fonplégade
Grand Cru Classé
T: 05 57 74 43 11, F: 05 57 74 44 67
Distinguished château producing
sound, juicy, hospitable, stylish wine.

Château Franc-Mayne
Grand Cru Classé
T: 05 57 24 62 61, F: 05 57 24 68 25
Nicely coloured, strong, elegant wine.

Château La Gaffelière
Premier Grand Cru Classé (B)
T: 05 57 24 72 15, F: 05 57 24 68 25
A supple, meaty St-Emilion matures in
the cellars opposite the large, slightly
gothic château.

baked according to a 17th-century recipe from Ursuline
sisters and are the town's only speciality – besides the wine
that is. The Place du Marché does offer some original and
attractive souvenirs, however, in the form of bonsai vines;
there are a number of varieties available.

In this square, too, there is the entrance to the *église
monolithe*, the biggest cave church in Europe. It was hewn
out by Benedictine monks in the 11th and 12th centuries.
There used to be frescos on its walls, but most of them
disappeared after the French Revolution, when the church
was not only stripped of its decorations and ornaments, but
was also used to store saltpetre. In 1837 the cave was brought
back into use. Today it is used only for special ceremonies
and functions, such as meetings of the Jurade. It is an
impressive, but also a rather austere, place, and smells of
damp and mould. Close to this monolithic church is the
little Chapelle de la Trinité and, below it, the cave where
Saint Aemilianus lived as a hermit. You can see the stone bed

Left *The entrance to Château Ausone. This is one of the two Premiers Grands Crus Classés of St-Emilion, the other being Château Cheval Blanc. Ausone produces deeply perfumed wines rivalling the greatest in the Médoc.*

Château Grand Mayne
T: 05 57 74 42 50, F: 05 57 24 68 34
A wine with concentration and quality.

Château Larmande
Grand Cru Classé
T: 05 57 24 71 41, F: 05 57 74 42 80
A pithy, slow-developing, quality wine.

Château Magdelaine
Premier Grand Cru Classé (B)
The interest here lies in the wine rather than the property. Magdelaine is hard to equal for flawless quality and a complete and generous taste with a style of its own. The vineyard is 80 per cent Merlot. Belongs to Jean-Pierre Moueix, a Libourne *négociant* that has the greater share in Château Pétrus in Pomerol, amongst others.

Château Mauvezin
Grand Cru Classé
T: 05 57 24 72 36, F: 05 57 74 48 54
Wine with a smooth solidity and some elegance too.

Château Pavie
Premier Grand Cru Classé (B)
T: 05 57 55 43 43, F: 05 57 24 63 99
On a southwest slope; limestone cellars have vine-roots growing through the ceiling. Stylish, supple fragrant wine.

Château Soutard
Grand Cru Classé
T: 05 57 24 72 23, F: 05 57 24 66 94
Elegant, likeable wine from large estate.

Château Troplong Mondot
Grand Cru Classé
T: 05 57 55 32 05, F: 05 57 55 32 07
Powerful wine with great elegance, a long finish and fine touches of wood.

Château Villemaurine
Grand Cru Classé
T: 05 57 74 46 44, F: 05 57 43 08 75
Generous, concentrated wine; meaty and rich. The splendid cellars host banquets as well as wine.

Couvent des Jacobins
Grand Cru Classé
T: 05 57 24 70 66, F: 05 56 24 92 51
Established in a former 13th-century monastery with splendid rock cellars. Outstanding, complete wine with strength, roundness, breeding, tannin, wood and fruit. Good for laying down.

the saint slept on, his altar, and the spring where he quenched his thirst. According to local legend, women could obtain a cure for their infertility by calling on the help of this saint.

The Rue de la Cadène, the little street that leads downhill from here, is cobbled with stones said to have been brought in as ballast by English ships sailing here from London to load up with wine.

High above the southern part of the little town rises the tower of Château du Roy. Every year the Jurade proclaims the start of the grape harvest from this castle, which has two-metre thick walls. It was built by Henry III of England and is the only surviving donjon, or keep, in the Gironde. In the higher, northern part of Saint-Emilion you can drink a glass of locally made sparkling wine amongst the ruins (and what is left of the cloisters) of the 14th-century Couvent des Cordeliers (Monastery of the Grey Friars). Nearby is the Porte de la Cadène, with its Gothic arches. Walking on

Above and below St-Emilion is full of historic details at every turn and is perfect for exploring on foot. Far right Macarons are a local speciality made from ground almonds, sugar and egg whites. Right Château Cheval Blanc is situated close to the boundary with Pomerol.

RECOMMENDED PRODUCERS: THE SURROUNDING VILLAGES

Château de Cantin
Grand Cru Classé
T: 05 57 24 65 73, F: 05 57 24 65 82
(St-Christophe-des-Bardes)
Partly barrel-aged wine with a captivating bouquet and an expansive taste, full of character. The château is a former 17th century monastry.

Château La Couronne
Grand Cru Classé
T: 05 56 56 04 59, F: 05 56 56 04 59
(St-Christophe-des-Bardes)
A rising star, since the firm of Mähler-Besse took over and renovated the cellars.

Château Fleur Cardinale
Grand Cru Classé
T: 05 57 40 14 05, F: 05 57 40 28 62
(St-Etienne-de-Lisse)
Usually offers wine of an intense colour, spicy oak, liquorice, fruit and firmness. One of the most respected *grands crus.*

northwards, you come to the Porte Bourgeoise, with the ruins of the Palais Cardinal close by. This Romanesque building was the residence of Cardinal de Saint-Luce, first dean of Saint-Emilion.

The surrounding villages
Saint-Emilion itself is the most important area, but not the only one covered by this appellation. Wines from eight other communes, or parts of them, can be sold under this name. Most tourists only make a point of visiting Saint-Emilion, but the other villages deserve to be seen too – not least because their settings are often attractive and they are frequently more peaceful. You could begin your tour

in Saint-Christophe-des-Bardes (*see* map on page 101), northeast of Saint-Emilion. It has a Romanesque church with many (rather weathered) sculptures and reliefs, and has been declared a historic monument. Here also is Château Laroque, one of the oldest in the district – as is clear from the medieval tower. The main building dates from the 18th century.

Nearby at Château Ferrande you can go underground – part of the system of passages to explore is prehistoric – and there is also a spring. Then there is Saint-Hippolyte's 14th-century village church, standing on a hill. You should now take the D245 to Saint-Etienne-de-Lisse, which has a fortified Romanesque church. The village is beautifully

situated at the foot of a limestone plateau. Continue the tour by following the D670 in the Libourne direction and then taking the turning to Saint-Sulpice-de-Faleyrens. The church at Saint-Sulpice is 11th-century. Between this church and Pierrefitte is Château Lescours, where a number of French kings have stayed, among them Henry of Navarre. North of Saint-Sulpice, near the little river harbour of Pierrefitte, is the best-preserved menhir in the *département*. It is a block of stone standing about five metres high and three metres wide, shaped like a hand, and more than 5,000 years old. Back in the immediate area of Saint-Emilion you can visit the hamlet of Saint-Martin-de-Mazerat, where there is a picturesque churchyard, and some renowned châteaux, such as Château Canon, nearby.

The wines

The Saint-Emilion wines – exclusively red – are relatively smooth in taste. Most of them are perfectly ready for drinking when they are young, but have sufficient backbone to mature for years in the bottle. The district has its own separate classification system. This was started in 1955 and has been revised a number of times since then. At the top come the *premiers grands cru classé* châteaux, within which group Château Ausone and Château Cheval Blanc enjoy a special status.

Château Fombrauge
Grand Cru Classé
T: 05 57 24 77 12, F: 05 57 24 66 95
(St-Christophe-des-Bardes)
Smooth, generous, reliable wine.

Château Haut Rocher
Grand Cru Classé
T: 05 57 40 18 09, F: 05 57 40 08 23
(St-Etienne-de-Lisse)
This estate has belonged to the same family since the 17th century. Its wine tends to be intense in colour and taste, and offers ageing potential.

Château Haut-Sarpe
Grand Cru Classé
T: 05 57 51 41 86, F: 05 57 51 76 83
(St-Christophe-des-Bardes)
Versailles-like château which in good years makes balanced, complex and delicious wines.

Château Monbousquet
(St-Sulpice-de-Faleyrens)
The wine is loaded with fruit and is of impeccable quality; deserves to be a Grand Cru Classé.

Château Bonnet
T: 05 57 47 15 23, F: 05 57 47 12 95
(St-Pey-d'Armens)
An excellent wine in its category, full of taste and of faultless quality.

Château Tertre Roteboeuf
T: 05 57 24 70 57, F: 05 57 74 42 11
(St-Laurent-des-Combes)
A massive colour, layers of fruit and great intensity, the wine here is impressive.

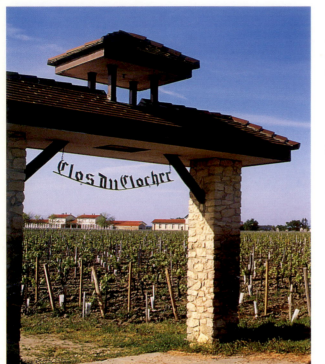

Pomerol

—··—··—	Canton boundary
—··—··—	Commune (parish) boundary
CHÂTEAU	Top-quality château
Château	Other good château
▉	First-growth vineyard
▉	Other vineyard
🌳	Woods
══25══	Contour interval 5 metres

Left *Clos du Clocher. This Pomerol property is situated on the high plateau, on deep gravelly soil. The wine is made using 50 per cent new oak.*

POMEROL

The Pomerol wine district is relatively small, but it is worked by as many as 175 growers. The average area of the holdings is therefore tiny: Château de Sales, Pomerol's largest estate, has 47.5 hectares. Despite the small scale, the appellation includes a number of world-famous wines. In fact Château Pétrus (the best of all the Pomerol châteaux) ranks alongside Château d'Yquem and Burgundy's La Romanée-Conti as one of the most expensive wines in the world, anywhere.

The eight small hamlets (or clusters of houses) that together make up the Pomerol commune are administered from Pomerol-Centre – recognisable from afar by its church steeple. This structure, with its 100 pillars, replaced the crumbling 12th-century church built by the Knights of Saint-John (later known as the Knights of Malta), the order which offered help and shelter to travellers and pilgrims at the time of the Crusades. Pomerol was a chosen base as it was on one of the pilgrim routes to Santiago de Compostela in the northwest of Spain. There are to this day signposts with Maltese crosses on them marking the old pilgrim way near the châteaux of Beauregard, Moulinet and La Commanderie, and at many other points. The Knights probably stimulated the growing of wine in the Pomerol region too, if only for its use in the Mass and as medicine. This would be why the local wine fraternity was named

Château
Mazeyres

Château
Clos Mazeyres

Beauséjour

Libourne

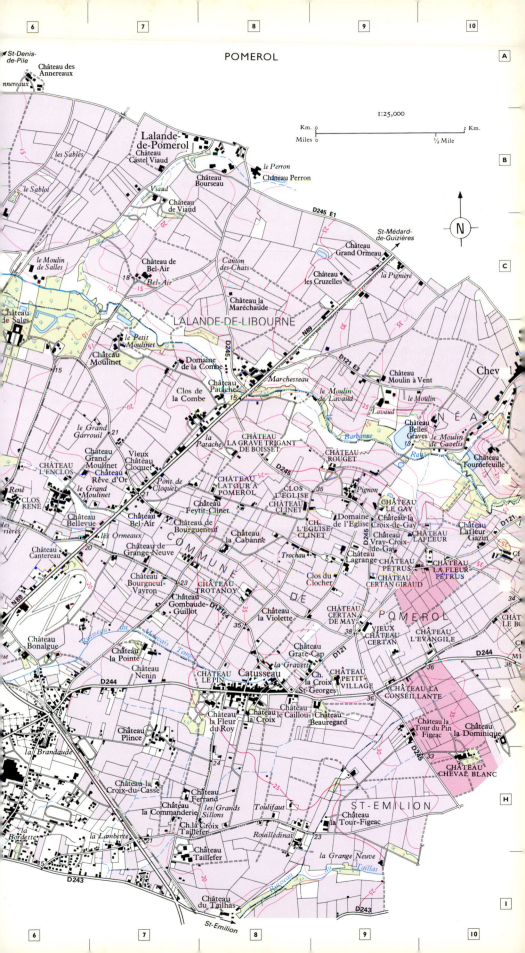

POMEROL

RECOMMENDED PRODUCERS

Château Beauregard
T: 05 57 51 13 36, F: 05 57 25 09 55
One of the few grand châteaux in
Pomerol, complete with moat, towers
and winding stairway. It dates from the
17th century. Beautiful wine.

Château Le Bon Pasteur
T: 05 57 51 10 94, F: 05 57 25 05 54
Generous, excellent wine made by
well-known oenologist, Michel Rolland.

**Château Certan de May de
Certan**
T: 05 57 51 41 53, F: 05 57 51 88 51
Exceptionally good Pomerol from a
small estate opposite Vieux Château
Certan. Wine of firmness and grace.

Château Clinet
T: 05 56 30 10 35, F: 05 56 30 11 45
Top-class Pomerol.

Château La Conseillante
T: 05 57 51 15 32, F: 05 57 51 42 39
Estate on the St-Emilion/Pomerol
boundary. Wine with a firm yet
exquisite, silky taste of great purity,
and a very fine, generous bouquet.

Château La Croix de Gay
T: 05 57 51 19 05, F: 05 57 74 15 62
Splendid wine with style and backbone.

Château l'Eglise Clinet
T: 05 57 25 99 00, F: 05 57 25 21 96
Richly nuanced wine with deep colour;
creamy, rounded and refined style.

Château l'Evangile
T: 05 57 51 15 30, F: 05 57 51 45 78
The vineyard (Rothschild-owned since
1990) borders on Château Pétrus
and makes a splendid, stylish Pomerol,
with a violet-like perfume.

Château La Fleur-Pétrus
T: 05 57 51 78 96, F: 05 57 51 79 79
Château with strikingly coloured
shutters. Complex wine.

Château Gazin
T: 05 57 51 07 05, F: 05 57 51 69 69
Very reliable

Château Petit-Village
T: 05 57 24 62 61, F: 05 57 24 68 25
Excellent Pomerol which is anything
but *petit*; plenty of fruit in its younger
years, with firm wood underneath.

La Confrérie des Hospitaliers, and
its members have the Maltese cross
depicted on their robes.

The taste of many Pomerols
makes a more homogeneous first
impression than is the case in the
wines of the other Bordeaux
districts. Most Pomerol wines
are more accessible in flavour,
more charming, warmer and less
reserved in style. And this is all despite the great many
variations in the region's soil structure.

In the heart of the district there is a plateau, about 35
metres high, with a superabundance of clay in its soil, mixed
in with gravel, forming an important square of vineyards.
Here, powerful, generous, richly coloured wines are
produced: Château Pétrus is the very best of them. Then
around this plateau there is a fairly narrow strip of gravel,
clay and sand. The wines from vines grown here are robust,
intense, but often less rounded and luxurious than those
from the plateau. Further west in the district the terrain is
flatter and sandier, and the result from these vineyards is
comparatively light, supple wines. Another variation in
many places is a hard, compact, iron-bearing layer of

sandstone in the subsoil. This is the *crasse de fer* which is renowned for the special qualities it lends to the wines coming from the vineyards it frequents – it is said to give Pomerols their sometimes truffle-like aroma.

The 17th-century Château Beauregard is a Pomerol wine estate well worth a visit. It was one of the first properties to arise in the region, and has an imposing château surrounded by a moat and (unusually for Pomerol) extensive grounds. In the 1920s an exact copy of it was built on Long Island for the Guggenheim family.

Château Pétrus
T: 05 57 51 78 96, F: 05 57 51 79 79
Pétrus, for all its fame, will disappoint anyone who is looking for a grand château – until you taste the wine. Pétrus is the Pomerol of Pomerols: a dark, exceptionally intense wine that overwhelms the senses with its power. Its unique class puts its price – three times the price of Médoc first-growths – beyond the reach of ordinary mortals. A Moueix team looks after the vineyard (95 per cent Merlot) and makes the wine (its other Pomerol properties include Feytit-Clinet, La Fleur-Pétrus, La Grave Trigant de Boisset, Lagrange, Latour à Pomerol and Trotanoy).

Château La Pointe
T: 05 57 51 02 11, F: 05 57 51 42 33
Extensive estate where two roads join – hence La Pointe. The château looks out over a magnificent park with stately old trees. Can make colourful, sinewy wines for laying down.

Château de Sales
T: 05 57 51 04 92, F: 05 57 25 23 91
Pomerol's biggest estate with an impressive château and extensive park. Always reliable wine with style, structure, elegance and fine perfume.

Château Trotanoy
T: 05 57 51 78 96, F: 05 57 51 79 79
Moueix estate on Pomerol's central plateau. The wine is grander than the country house château: concentrated, deep-coloured, with smooth fruit and meaty power. If Pétrus is the emperor of Pomerol, Trotanoy is the king.

Château La Violette
T: 05 57 51 49 78, F: 05 57 51 60 34
Delicious wine, with a fragrance of violets. A feminine, stylish Pomerol that lingers nicely.

Château Vray-Croix-de-Gay
T: 05 57 51 64 58, F: 05 57 51 41 56
Less well-known, intense, elegant wine.

Vieux Château Certan
T: 05 57 51 17 33, F: 05 57 25 35 08
The oldest known winery in Pomerol – 16th century. A flawless, charming, stylish wine is made, gaining in fragrance and complexity with time. Easily recognised by its pink cap.

Top left *Château La Pointe.*
Top *Château La Croix de Gay. In recent years investment in installations and expertise has greatly improved the quality of this château's wines.*

Above *Crusty loaves of bread – a French staple.*
Left *Sheep grazing alongside vineyards in the outlying parts of Pomerol. Sights like this are rare because vines are so widespread in the Libournais.*

ST-EMILION SATELLITES

HOTEL

Château de Roques
T: 05 57 74 62 18
In Puisseguin, offering an attractive
chambre d'hôte amongst the vineyards.

RECOMMENDED PRODUCERS

LUSSAC-ST-EMILION
Château de Barbe Blanche
T: 05 56 63 27 66, F: 05 56 76 87 03
Glorious, rounded, truly substantial wine.
Château du Courlat
T: 05 57 51 62 17, F: 05 57 51 28 28
(Libourne)
Old vine Jean Baptiste *cuvée is* richly
structured, refined, yet powerful.
Château Mayne-Blanc
T: 05 57 74 60 56, F: 05 57 74 51 77
Satisfyingly mouth-filling St-Vincent
cuvée, with good tannins on the finish.

MONTAGNE-ST-EMILION
Château Calon
T: 05 57 51 64 88, F: 05 57 51 56 30
Charming wine, of high quality.
Château Maison Blanche
T: 05 57 74 62 18, F: 05 57 74 58 98
Reliable, well-structured wine with
smooth finish, rich in tannin.
Château Roudier
T: 05 57 74 62 06, F: 05 57 74 59 34
Pleasant, lingering wine with plenty of
juice in the taste.
Vieux Château St-André
T: 05 57 51 75 55, F: 05 57 25 13 30
(Libourne)
Wine from one of the greatest
Libournais oenologists, Jean Claude
Berrouet. Great Montagne-St-Emilion.

PUISSEGUIN-ST-EMILION
Château Branda
T: 05 57 74 62 55, F: 05 57 74 57 33
Barrel-aged wine of consistent quality.
Château Durand-Laplagne
T: 05 57 74 63 07, F: 05 57 74 63 07
The Cuvée Sélection is beautifully
coloured, with a good, long finish
marked by its wood.

THE SAINT-EMILION SATELLITES

Across the Barbanne stream, which forms the northern boundary of both Saint-Emilion and Pomerol, lie the so-called satellite districts: the villages of Lussac, Montagne, Puisseguin and Saint-Georges. Each is allowed to couple its name with that of Saint-Emilion. Parsac used to be among them but was subsequently incorporated into Montagne–Saint-Emilion.

Lussac-Saint-Emilion

Lussac lies nine kilometres from Saint-Emilion. In its centre there is a remarkable representation of an atom made from wine casks: it is rather less than beautiful. What *is* attractive is the Maison du Vin, in a 19th-century building with vaulting and oak beams. Also worth seeing is the village church, with a bas–relief of harvest scenes. Lussac hosts an unusual sporting event: the international barrel-rolling triathlon where oak wine casks are propelled along in spectacular fashion. The contest takes place on the second Saturday in September, and a craft fair and flea–market is held on the Sunday. There is also a weekly market on Thursdays. Other places worth visiting are Château Lussac and the Picampeau menhir – known as Pierre des Martyrs – once used as a sacrificial stone.

Montagne-Saint-Emilion

This is by far the most important of the satellite districts, at least in volume. In the middle of the little village there is a striking church with curious heads over

the main door. Standing on the church steps here, you are precisely level with the weather-vane of Saint-Emilion's church (Montagne is on a considerable hill).

In the village, next to the Maison du Vin, there is a wine museum, the Eco-Musée du Vigneron-Paysan. Here you can learn everything about wine and winegrowing... '*tout sur les petites misères et les grands mystères du vin, de la vigne et du vigneron*'.

Puisseguin-Saint-Emilion

The landscape from Lussac to Puisseguin is beautiful, evoking visions of Tuscany with its many hills and groves of cypress trees. The name Puisseguin comes from Puy, meaning 'hill', and Seguin, one of Charlemagne's warriors who settled here in about AD 800. Viticulture dates from some 1,000 years later. The little village is more than usually rustic – the Maison du Vin acts as a tobacconist's, too.

Saint-Georges-Saint-Emilion

The growers of this, the smallest of the satellites, have the choice of using the Montagne-Saint-Emilion appellation or their own. The best wine comes from the finest château for miles around: Château Saint-Georges – a splendid example of Louis XVI architecture. It shows a striking resemblance to the Grand Théâtre in Bordeaux, built in 1770 by the same architect, Victor Louis. The château dominates its surroundings and you can often take your bearings from it as you explore. Saint-Georges itself has a rather exceptional 12th-century church with two storeys, built in Romanesque style on Roman ruins. Notice also the four-storey belltower. The *jardin du curé*, beside this, has some unusual plants.

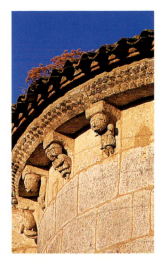

Far left Farm-fresh local cheese available from most local markets. Above The church in St-Georges. Below Vines stretch over Puisseguin-St-Emilion.

Château Lafaurie
T: 05 57 24 33 66, F: 05 57 24 30 42
After undergoing extensive changes and renovations, this estate now makes a strong wine with plenty of tannin.
Château des Laurets
T: 05 57 74 63 40, F: 05 57 74 65 34
This is a firmly-structured, tannic wine from an extensive estate, with a big château.

ST-GEORGES-ST EMILION
Château Belair St-Georges
T: 05 57 74 65 40, F: 05 57 74 51 51
(Montagne)
Fine balanced wine that needs a few years.
Château Cap d'Or
T: 05 57 40 08 88, F: 05 57 40 19 93
Well-made juicy wine with a light touch of wood.
Château St-Georges
T: 05 57 74 62 11, F: 05 57 74 58 62
(Montagne)
The noblest wine of the district; rich, with strength and a generous constitution. The château is impressive and one of the most beautiful on the west bank.
Château Tour du Pas St-Georges
T: 05 57 24 70 94, F: 05 57 24 67 11
Note the two remarkable wood sculptures outside the cellar. The wine is made by the team of Château Ausone.

COTES DE CASTILLON

HOTEL

Hostellerie du Château Lardier
T: 05 57 40 54 11, F: 05 57 40 72 35
Pleasant, quiet hotel/restaurant in the
hamlet of Ruch. Good rooms from
FF260. No restaurant.

RESTAURANTS

La Péniche
T: 05 57 40 30 30
Simple restaurant on the quay beside
the Dordogne. Tasty lunch from FF100.

SPECIAL INTEREST

The annual Castillon-la-Bataille wine
fair is usually held in the second half
of July. This village also has a Maison
du Vin, where details about visits to
châteaux can be obtained.

Just outside Castillon, to the east,
stands the chapel the French
commanders had built in honour of
John Talbot, the English leader who
fell here in 1453. The battle between
the French and the English is
re-enacted each year at Belvès-de-
Castillon, a little to the north; you can
drive there on the D119.

RECOMMENDED PRODUCERS

BELVES-DE-CASTILLON
Château Castegens
T: 05 57 47 96 07, F: 05 57 47 91 61
Worth tasting in this ancient castle is
the cask-aged Cuvée Spéciale

Above *Food being prepared in
a simple kitchen in the village of
Montagne-St-Emilion.*
Right *A view of a vineyard in the
Côtes de Francs, east of St-Emilion.
This beautiful area, granted its
appellation in 1967, now produces
some high-quality wines.*
Below *The charming courtyard of
the Château de Francs.*

COTES DE CASTILLON

On July 17th 1453 near Castillon, a decisive battle was fought
between the French and the English. The latter had the worst
of it and Aquitaine became French again after three centuries.
In 1953 Castillon commemorated the 500th anniversary of
this encounter, and 'la Bataille' was added to its name.

Castillon was once an important river port: a fortified
town with a large fortress. But only near the Porte de Fer,
on the south side by the river, can remains of the town walls
be seen. Castillon's church dates from the 18th century, and
the *mairie* occupies what was once a hospital.

Today, there is a French airforce base near Saint-Philippe d'Aiguilhe: its radio masts can be seen for miles. Of greater interest, however, is the water tower nearby, open for the public to climb for a marvellous view of the whole region.

Another vantage point is located at Sainte-Colombe. Getting there from Saint-Philippe-d'Aiguilhe you can pass through Saint-Genès-de-Castillon, with a stately 15th-century house. Finally, at Saint-Magne-de-Castillon, northwest of Castillon-la-Bataille, there is another church worth seeing.

Castillon wines were elevated from Bordeaux Supérieur to their own appellation in 1989. They rather resemble those of the Saint-Emilion Satellite districts.

COTES DE FRANCS

Côtes de Francs is a small district taking its name from the village of Francs. The oldset parts of its castle – the Château de Francs – date from the 12th century, the rest from the 14th and 17th centuries. Two Saint-Emilion families produce some notable wines.

Just north of Francs is the hamlet of Tayac, where the remains of a Gallo-Roman settlement have been found and there is a Romanesque church. If you then head south on the D123, it is not far to Saint-Cibard, where there are two leading wine properties (Puyguéraud and Laclaverie); the church here is 12th century. West of Saint-Cibard, on a hill near Monbadon, stands a 14th-century feudal castle.

STE-COLOMBE
Château Poupille
T: 05 57 74 43 03, F: 05 57 74 45 12
Wine with a complex aroma, tremendously rich in style and tannins. Long, balanced aftertaste with fruit.
Château Lapeyronie
T: 05 57 40 19 27, F: 05 57 40 14 38
Top-class wine.

ST-MAGNE-DE-CASTILLON
Château Peyrou
T: 05 57 24 72 05, F: 05 57 74 40 03
Excellent wine from vines more than 40 years old.

ST-PHILIPPE-D'AGUILHE
Château d'Aguilhe
T: 05 57 40 60 10, F: 05 57 40 63 56
Old ruins, delicious wines.
Château Lamartine
A fine bouquet with a slightly 'animal' hint to it, a pleasing palate with a suggestion of chocolate, and a long, concentrated aftertaste.

LES SALLES-DE-CASTILLON
Château de Belcier
T: 05 57 40 62 90, F: 05 57 40 64 25
Full-bodied wine, one of the best in the district. Château dates from 1790.

COTES DE FRANCS

RECOMMENDED PRODUCERS

FRANCS
Château de Francs
T: 05 57 40 65 91, F: 05 57 40 63 04
Interesting wine with a rich aroma of red fruits and fine, smooth tannin in the aftertaste.

ST-CIBARD
Château Laclaverie
T: 05 57 40 63 76, F: 05 57 40 66 08
This is the property of Nicolas Thienpont, who makes simply amazing wine here.
Château Puyguéraud
T: 05 57 40 61 04, F: 05 57 40 66 08
Adjoins Laclaverie and is also owned by the Thienpont family. The wine is subtle and elegant, with rich, perfumed aromas.

LALANDE-DE-POMEROL

RECOMMENDED PRODUCERS

Château de Bel-Air
T: 05 57 51 40 07, F: 05 57 74 17 43
Balanced wine with soft fruit.
Château Grand Ormeau
T: 05 57 25 30 20, F: 05 57 25 22 80
This is a deeply coloured, sensual wine that has an attractive touch of wood.

Château de Viaud
T: 05 57 51 17 86, F: 05 57 51 79 77
One of the oldest estates in Lalande.
Fine, robust wine with a lovely
bouquet and a firm finish.
Château Haut-Chaigneau
T: 05 57 74 62 25, F: 05 57 74 51 04
(Néac)
Always hospitable, and good wines.

Château les Hauts-Conseillants
T: 05 57 51 62 17, F: 05 57 51 28 28
(Néac)
An estate where traditional methods
are followed, with flawless results.
Wonderfully aromatic; delicious hints
of vanilla, spices and black fruit. A
beautiful wine for laying down.
Château Les Templiers
T: 05 57 51 70 27, F: 05 57 51 60 34
(Néac)
Well-structured wine.

LALANDE-DE-POMEROL

This appellation is intended only for wines produced in the communes of Lalande and Néac. These two villages lie north of Pomerol and Saint-Emilion and are separated from them by a little stream, the Barbanne. To the east and south they border on Montagne-Saint-Emilion.

Lalande-de-Pomerol (which is another of the towns on the pilgrimage routes to Santiago de Compostela) has been associated with wine since the 10th or 11th century. The fine little church, with a curious open belfry, dates from a short time after this, in the 12th century; a little more recently again, in the churchyard, stands a cross from the 1400s. The church is the only building here that has a history as far back as the time of the Knights of the Holy Cross, and painted in the nave is a list of their rules. Château des Templiers nearby is yet further evidence of their presence.

Lalande wines at one time were classified under Pomerol's appellation, while those of Néac had the designation Néac-Pomerol. Legislation in the 1920s changed this, giving rise to the appellation Lalande-de-Pomerol, and taking away Néac's right to use the Pomerol name. Formally speaking, the separate Néac appellation still exists, although it is no longer applied in practice because in 1954 it was decided that Néac could use the Lalande-de-Pomerol name. The wines of Lalande-de-Pomerol are usually rather less generous, less noble than those of Pomerol, but are clearly related to them – and cost much less.

Above   The Domaine de l'Eglise produces highly structured and richly flavoured Pomerol.
Right   A change from vines – woods in the Côtes de Castillon.
Far right   The church of Lalande-de-Pomerol.

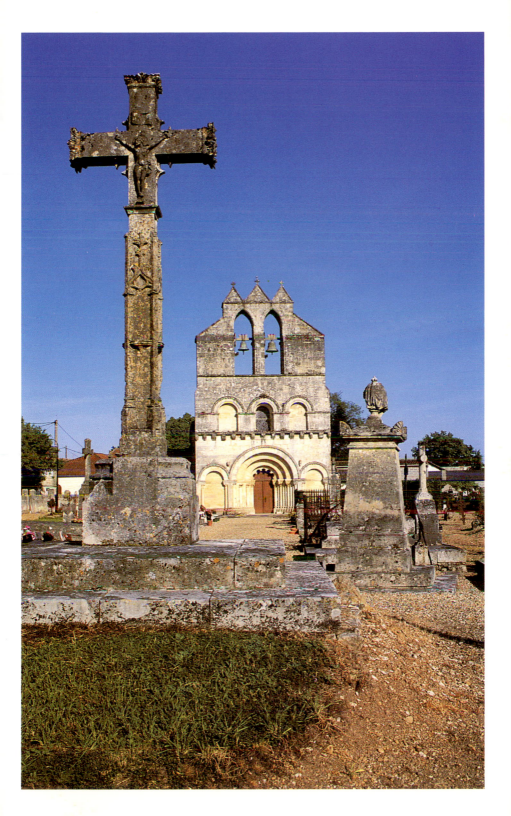

FRONSAC

RESTAURANTS

Le Bord d'Eeau
T: 05 57 51 99 91
Restaurant by the Dordogne on the
D670, the best of the district.
Lunchtime menus start below FF100.

RECOMMENDED PRODUCERS

FRONSAC
Château Barrabaque
T: 05 57 51 31 79, F: 05 57 25 32 83
The Prestige Cuvée is remarkable.
Château La Marche-Canon
T: 05 57 64 23 67, F: 05 57 64 36 20
The Candelaire is made from very
old vines only and is a formidable
Canon-Fronsac.
Château Moulin Pey-Labrie
T: 05 57 51 14 37, F: 05 57 51 53 45
A great wine with a rounded,
muscular and harmonious taste.
Château La Grave
T: 05 57 51 31 11, F: 05 57 25 08 61
Balanced wine with wood, tannin,
juice and style, from a grower with
totally ecological principles.

LA RIVIERE
Château de la Rivière
T: 05 57 55 56 56, F: 05 57 24 94 39
A formidable wine, powerful and rich
in tannin on the palate. The quality
reaches at least the level of the better
Médoc *crus bourgeois*.

SAILLANS
Château Moulin Haut-Laroque
T: 05 57 84 32 07, F: 05 57 84 31 84
Distinguished Fronsac with a
spectrum of flavours.
Château Dalem
T: 05 57 84 34 18, F: 05 57 74 39 85
A great wine with a deep colour
and rich aroma of red fruit and
liquorice. Also castle from the
18th century.
Château Villars
T: 05 57 84 32 17, F: 05 57 84 31 25
Concentrated, noble wine.

ST-MICHEL-DE-FRONSAC
Château Canon
Wine of an unmistakable elegance.
Château Cassagne Haut-Canon
T: 05 57 51 63 98, F: 05 57 51 62 20
The regular wine has an agreeably
fruity nose, and a rounded taste with
a slight hint of wood; the Cuvée La
Truffière is more complex.

FRONSAC

Near the ancient village of Fronsac, just west of Libourne, a
hill rises steeply, fortified at separate points in history by the
Gauls and the Romans. Charlemagne built a stronghold on
it, which in the following centuries first fulfilled a military
function and then became a traffic control point, the owners
levying tolls on vessels passing by on the River Dordogne.
The castle has been gone now since the 17th century; what
remains is a splendid view across Fronsac, numerous
châteaux, the river valley, and part of Entre-Deux-Mers.

Anyone driving up or down this hill will pass the Fronsac
Maison du Vin, with plenty of information about the local
wines and visits to châteaux. Wine is sold here, too.

Fronsac's Romanesque church is an historic monument,
and the village has some beautiful buildings to watch out for,
dating from the 17th and other centuries past. Behind
Fronsac there lies a romantic winegrowing countryside with
winding roads, hills, châteaux, and ever-changing distant
views. That viticulture here dates from Roman times is very
clear from the remains of one of that period's villas in Saint-
Aignan. This hamlet also has a Romanesque church.

Château Mazéris
T: 05 57 24 96 93, F: 05 57 24 98 25
Seductive wines wrapped in velvety
fruit.
Château Mazéris-Bellevue
T: 05 57 24 98 19, F: 05 57 24 90 32
Some people compare this wine to a
good Médoc.

The Château de la Rivière, in the west of the Fronsac district, is a large, originally 13th-century castle flanked by two square towers. It was built against a high, well-wooded slope and is very much geared to receiving visitors. The view from the château is glorious. The cellars behind the castle where the wines are aged make an almost Wagnerian impact. Visitors pay for admission, but can retrieve this fee when they buy a few bottles here.

Main picture *Sun shines on a quiet street in the village of Puisseguin.*
Above *Vines at Château de la Rivière, which dates from the 13th century. This is one of Fronsac's most important properties, both visually and in terms of fine wine production.*

Adjoining the Fronsac district there is a second, smaller area called Canon-Fronsac. In the former there are around 120 producers active; in the latter 50 or so. The Fronsac wines were unknown for a long time, but many growers invested a great deal in them during the 1980s, and a sometimes spectacular improvement in quality has been the result. In the matter of wine, Fronsac and Canon-Fronsac have many a surprise in store.

The East Bank of the Gironde

The River Gironde separates two wine districts on its east bank from the Médoc: Côtes de Bourg, and Blaye to the north of it. Both regions take their names from former fortress towns. Blaye was the more important of the two and today is livelier than Bourg, which gives a rather sleepy impression. It is the red wines of Côtes de Bourg, however, that have had the better reputation in the past. But thanks to present ideas of winegrowing and vinification, both regions are regarded as having equal quality and worth. There is also white Côtes de Bourg, but this amounts to only five per cent of the region's production. The proportions are quite different in Blaye, for although red wines also predominate here, whites account for 20 per cent of production. The white wines of Blaye enjoy a particularly good reputation. In general they are not wines of any great refinement, but are easy-drinking and are pleasant when they are young. There are nevertheless some surprising exceptions to this rule, and their number is growing steadily but surely.

Bourg lies only 15 kilometres from Blaye. It is easiest to begin a visit to the two districts in Bourg, which is nearer to Bordeaux.

Left The historical town of Bourg with the castle in the foreground. Bourg's strategic importance on the River Gironde was first recognised by the Romans; in its time it has been a major fort and a harbour.

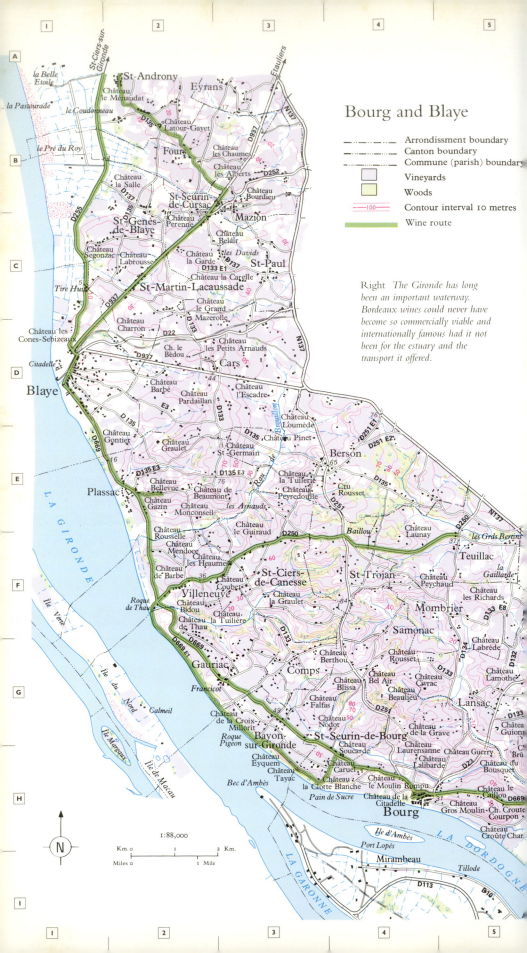

Bourg and Blaye

Arrondissment boundary
Canton boundary
Commune (parish) boundary
Vineyards
Woods
Contour interval 10 metres
Wine route

Right The Gironde has long been an important waterway. Bordeaux wines could never have become so commercially viable and internationally famous had it not been for the estuary and the transport it offered.

1:88,000

Km. 0   1   2 Km.
Miles 0   1 Mile

N

COTES DE BOURG

The hilly landscape of the Côtes de Bourg is referred to as 'the Switzerland of the Gironde'. The district lies on the right bank of the River Dordogne, close to the point where it becomes the Gironde. This charming countryside of rolling hillsides is home to some very agreeable wines, most of which are red.

To reach the Côtes de Bourg district from Bordeaux you can begin on the A10, travelling as far as the Saint-André-de-Cubzac exit and then turning off onto the D669. Another possibility is to go via the D911: this is not so quick perhaps, but has the advantage of taking you through an area that is otherwise apt to be forgotten. The bridge over the Dordogne, built by Gustave Eiffel, is one of the great sights on this route. To the left of the bridge is the Bec d'Ambès industrial complex, on a spit of land formed naturally by alluvial deposits.

After reaching the Côtes de Bourg on the D669 from Saint-André-de-Cubzac (where good Bordeaux and Bordeaux Supérieur wines are produced), there are a number of sights

to see. In Prignac–et–Marcamps there is the Pair–non–Pair cave with some 60 prehistoric wall paintings of animals – horses, bison, mammoth and ibex. The cave was discovered in 1881. Within this same commune are the Marcamps quarries. The Prignac district was once an important supplier of limestone, a large proportion of it shipped out from the harbour at Bourg.

If you turn right off the D669 onto the D133, you will soon be in Tauriac, where there is a fine, beautifully restored Romanesque church. There is a large, very active wine cooperative here too.

To visit Bourg, the best way now is to go back to the D669. The official name of this little town used to be Bourg-sur-Gironde, but this is no longer accurate: Bourg is now on the River Dordogne, not on the Gironde, due to the silting up of the river and the formation of the Bec d'Ambès which divides the two waterways.

COTES DE BOURG

 HOTEL

ST-CIERS-DE-CANESSE
La Closérie des Vignes
T: 05 57 64 81 90, F: 05 57 64 94 44
Very quiet, pleasantly comfortable, charming service. Simple, no-nonsense regional cuisine. Rooms from around FF450, meals from FF140. Swimming pool.

 RESTAURANTS

VIRSAC
Château Julie
T: 05 57 43 95 75
Wine estate with nine comfortable rooms and two separate apartments. Breakfast and winetastings included. Tennis court, swimming pool. From about FF525.

BOURG
Brassserie Le Plaisance
T: 05 57 68 45 34
For a simple lunch on a shadowed triangular terrace near the port (and the cooperative). Inexpensive, good value for money.
Le Troque Sel
T: 05 57 68 30 67
Simple restaurant near the Maison du Vin. Tasty food; set menus from FF100.

ST-GERVAIS
Au Sarment
T: 05 57 43 44 73
Congenial, rustic restaurant with a leafy terrace. Classic dishes with a modern touch, such as *poêlée d'huîtres au jus de truffes* and beef with a sturgeon *sabayon*. Not really cheap, but good. Set menus from around FF250.

Top *Seafood is plentiful in this part of the Bordeaux region due to its situation on the Gironde.*
Above *One of many charming bars and restaurants in the Côtes de Bourg and Blaye.*

Left *The imposing ancient battlements in Bourg are a dramatic reminder of the region's violent past, when, for centuries, it was fought over by the French and British.*

LE RIGALET
La Filadière
T: 05 57 64 94 05
In this small hamlet on the river there are several restaurants. This is the most attractive, with the best river view and the largest terrace. Set menus start under FF100; Sunday lunch costs around FF150. *Fruits de mer* are a speciality.

RECOMMENDED PRODUCERS

Château Falfas
T: 05 57 64 80 41, F: 05 57 64 93 24
(Bayon)
Château in Louis XIII-style and wines full of concentration.

Château Caruel
T: 05 57 68 43 07, F: 05 57 68 24 97
(Bourg)
Juicy, meaty wine with a good balance and a long finish.

Château de la Grave
T: 05 57 68 41 49, F: 05 57 68 99 26
(Bourg)
Reliable wines, made in a fairy-tale château.

Château Roc de Cambes
T: 05 57 68 25 58, F: 05 57 68 35 97
(Bourg)
Top quality wine. A superstar of Côtes de Bourg.

Château Le Clos du Notaire
T: 05 57 68 44 36, F: 05 57 68 32 87
(Bourg)
On average the wine matures for a year in casks; its quality is exceptional in good years.

Château La Croix-Davids
T: 05 57 68 40 05, F: 05 57 63 24 82
(Bourg)
A Côtes de Bourg with much
Cabernet Franc.

Château Haut-Guiraud
T: 05 57 64 91 39, F: 05 57 64 88 05
(St-Ciers-de-Caresse)
Sound, mouthfilling wine.

Château Macay
T: 05 57 68 41 50, F: 05 57 68 35 23
(Samonac)
Wine of a deep but vital red that, in
its smooth bouquet and lingering
taste, gives an impression of sweet
fruit. Delightful, especially in its youth.

Château Rousset
T: 05 57 68 46 34, F: 05 57 68 36 18
(Samonac)
Smooth elements of new wood give
the Grande Réserve a taste, with
spicy oak and vanilla.

Château Brulésecaille
T: 05 57 68 40 31, F: 05 57 68 21 27
(Tauriac)
Suitably broad taste, not without
tannin, and lingers well. An extremely
pleasant, very good Côtes de Bourg
that has justly won gold medals.

Château Guerry
T: 05 57 68 20 78, F: 05 57 68 41 31
(Tauriac)
Elegant, balanced wine
with backbone and a clean taste.
Among the best in the district.

Top *The pretty village of
Marmisson, near Blaye, which has
a prehistoric site.*
Above *Although wine tourism in
this part of Bordeaux is
undeveloped, the places of interest
are always well signposted.*
Right *An artist paints the view
across the Gironde estuary.*

Part of Bourg is on a steep chalk
escarpment close to the river: a good
defensive position and an unsurprising
location for Roman fortifications – later
these were extended to the whole of
Bourg. As a harbour it was once more
important even than Bordeaux. There is
not much left to see of all that history
today. The little town consists of an upper
and a lower area. In the upper part there
is the Maison du Vin and two adjoining
squares with terraces giving a view across
the Dordogne and the Bec d'Ambès; the lower town is also
a pleasant place to look around. The Château de la Citadelle
used to be occupied by the archbishops of Bordeaux and
now functions as a museum. Beneath it there is a maze of
underground passageways. Also in the lower part of the
town there are some fine houses, as well as a wine shop and
the growers' syndicate.

Not far from Bourg, to the west, is the hamlet of Pain-
du-Sucre where the sparkling wine Crémant de Bordeaux is
produced. In the Blaye direction there is a charming route

to follow that runs close to the riverbank (it meets up with the D669 again before you get to Blaye). You could also stay on the D669, or further explore the wine country of the Côtes de Bourg. The scenery is often lovely, with romantic, vine-clad valleys between the hills. In Teuillac, in the north of the district, there are also 9th-century tombs.

PREMIERES COTES DE BLAYE

Between Bourg and Blaye, about three kilometres south of the latter, is Plassac, where the remains of a Gallo-Roman villa can still be seen. A Gallo-Roman museum has been set up on the site, but it is open only from June to the end of September. Also at Plassac is the Butte de Montuzet, high ground which you can climb for a fine panoramic view of the surrounding countryside. In the village, you should take the road that ascends to Château Bellevue, and do the last bit to the top on foot.

Blaye is also dominated by a hill, albeit a much lower one. The Romans built a fortification here, which they called Blavia. Later, a castle rose on the same spot, but this was largely destroyed in the medieval period. The hill is now adorned with a vast citadel, built on the orders of Louis XIV to defend the Gironde against foreign invaders. This stronghold formed a defensive chain with similar forts on the island of Paté in the River Gironde and at Cussac in the Médoc. The architect was Vauban in all cases. The citadel only saw action on one occasion. Later, the revenue service had an office here, as any foreign ship wanting to go to

Château Haut-Macô
T: 05 57 68 81 26, F: 05 57 68 91 97
(Tauriac)
The Cuvée Year Bernard is full of nuances.

Château Tour des Graves
T: 05 57 64 32 02, F: 05 57 64 23 94
(Teuillac)
One of the rare good white wines from the Côtes de Bourg, with an almost exotic taste.

Château Mercier
T: 05 57 64 92 34, F: 05 57 64 83 37
(Trojan)
Superior wines.

Château de Mendoce
T: 05 57 68 34 95, F: 05 57 68 34 91
(Villeneuve)
A good Côtes de Bourg from a stately, well-preserved 15th and 16th-century castle. The highest quality is represented by the Cuvée Speciale.

BLAYE

HOTELS

La Citadelle
T: 05 57 42 17 10, F: 05 57 42 10 34
A good address, in the fortress itself, with a superb panoramic view across the Gironde. Has some 20 homely rooms from around FF300. The cuisine is regionally oriented with a modern touch. Many fish specialities, including *lamproie Bordelaise*. Set menus start at about FF150.

L'Olifant
T: 05 57 42 22 96, F: 05 57 42 34 07
Comfortable hotel/restaurant near
the D937 to Bordeaux (in St.-Martin-
Lacaussade). Simple cooking with a
set menu below FF100. The twelve
rooms cost less than FF400.

RECOMMENDED PRODUCERS

Château Peyredoulle
T: 05 57 64 39 63, F: 05 57 64 36 20
(Berson)
Red wine that is delightful when
young, with small red fruits in the
fragrance and taste; and the
suppleness is there quite early on.

Château Crusquet Sabourin
T: 05 57 42 15 27, F: 05 57 42 05 47
(Cars)
A generous wine with good
underlying wood and tannin.

*Above Blaye's almost perfectly
preserved citadel sits high above the
harbour, where the ferry crosses the
Gironde to Lamarque.*

*Right and below right Simple
but beautiful buildings are found in
Blaye, and there are delightful views
of the Gironde across to the Médoc.*

Bordeaux had to pay an 'entry fee' at Blaye. And, right up
to the French Revolution, English crews had to surrender
their weapons here. Although large parts of the citadel badly
need restoration, the structure today still remains most
impressive. It covers an area of 18 hectares and its walls
encompass a camping site, a hotel/restaurant, gardens, a
monastery with a chapel, a hospital and all necessary
security, including entrances. According to tradition, it is
said the grave of Roland, Charlemagne's nephew, lies
somewhere beneath the structure. He is said to have
been buried in AD 778 in a church then on the site.
There is also a museum of local history and art in the
citadel. As might be expected, there are fine views to
be had from the Tour de l'Aiguillette here.

The little town of Blaye itself is made up of
straight streets and small squares beside a still-busy
harbour, and has an industrious air. The local
economy is partly dependent on the presence of a
nuclear power station about 20 kilometres to the
north at Braud-et-Saint-Louis (this can be visited
by appointment, telephone: 05 57 33 32 03).

At Saint-Seurin-de-Cursac, also north of
Blaye, there is a museum of prehistory open in the
summer at the Château Rolland-Lagarde. In Saint-
Ciers-sur-Gironde there is a Romanesque church.

Château Gardut Haut-Cluzeau
T: 05 57 42 33 04, F: 05 57 42 08 92
(Cars)
Supple red wine that has deservedly
won many medals.

Château du Grand Barrail
T: 05 57 42 33 04, F: 05 57 42 08 92
(Cars)
Classic red wine with a pleasing
element of wood and a delicious
finish. The Blayais Sauvignon MP is
expressive. Same owner as Gardut
Haut-Cluzeau.

Château Marinier
T: 05 57 68 63 13, F: 05 57 68 18 08
(Cézac)
Excellent red Cuvée Prestige.

Château Haut Bertinerie
T: 05 57 68 70 74, F: 05 57 60 01 03
(Cubnezais)
Top class red Premières Côtes de
Blaye, with juice, some wood and
sufficient tannin. The white is
impressive too.

Château Haut-Grelot
T: 05 57 32 65 98, F: 05 57 32 71 81
(St-Ciers-sur-Gironde)
Red and white wines both merit
attention.

Château Charron
T: 05 57 42 66 66, F: 05 57 64 36 20
(St-Martin-la-Caussade)
Exemplary wine – both the red
(Premières Côtes de Blaye) and the
white (Acacia, a Côtes de Blaye).

Château Les Jonqueyres
T: 05 57 42 34 88, F: 05 57 42 93 80
(St-Paul-de-Blaye)
One of the best estates in this region.

Once you are back in Blaye,
a visit to the Maison du Vin
is well worthwhile. It is
situated in the centre of
town, on the Cours Vauban.
You will find friendly staff
there, and you will be able
to buy regional wines by the
bottle or case at very
reasonable prices.

Various appellations are in
force in Blaye. The red
wines, fairly light and often with a fresh taste to them, are
nearly always sold as Premières Côtes de Blaye; the
refreshing whites usually have the Côtes de Blaye
appellation, or sometimes Blayais.

GAZETTEER

Château

Maurens 101 F8
Mausse, le 100 C1
Mauvezin 107 E6
Mayne-Blanc 101 A8
Mayne, du, Barsac 83 B8
Mayne, du, Preignac 83 E8
Mayne, le 101 D9
Mayne-Vieil, le 100 A2
Mazeris 100 C2
Mazeyres 114 F5
Ménaudat, le 128 A2
Mendoce 128 F2
Menota, de 83 B8
Meyney 37 F9
Meynieu, le 36 F5
Mille Secousses, de 129 I6
Mission Haut-Brion, la 71 A6
Moines, des 100 B5
Monbadon, de 101 C10
Monbousquet 100 F5
Monbrison 60 F5
Moncets 100 C5
Monconseil 128 E2
Mondou 100 B5
Montaiguillon 101 C6
Montbrun 61 B6
Monthil 2 C3
Montlabert 106 D3
Montrose 37 G9
Morin 37 E7
Mouleyre, la 101 E9
Moulin-à-Vent, Listrac-
  Médoc 54 I1
Moulin à Vent, Pomerol
  100 C5, 115 D9
Moulin Blanc, Lussac 101 C8
Moulin-Blanc, Néac 101 C6
Moulin-de-Cadet 106 D4
Moulin-de-Castillon 3 D7
Moulin de Courrech 101 C9
Moulin-de-la-Rose 48 D6
Moulin des Laurets 101 D9
Moulinet 115 D7
Moulin Pey-Labrie 100 C1
Moulin-Riche 49 B4
Moulin Rompu, le 128 H4
Moulin-Rose 55 E6
Moulin Rouge, du 54 B4
Moulins de Calon 101 C7
Moulin St-Georges 106 G5
Moulis 54 I2
Mouton-Rothschild 43 D8
Musset, Lalande-de-
  Pomerol 100 B5
Musset, Montagne 101 D8
Myrat 83 B7
Nairac 83 A8
Négrit 101 C7
Nenin 100 C4, 115 G7
Nodot 128 G3
Nodoz 129 G6
Notton-Baury 60 D5
Olivier 71 F6
Ormes-de-Pez, Les- 37 E7
Ormes Sorbet, les 2 D5
Pabeau 3 H6
Pailhas 101 F7
Palmer 60 B5
Panigon 2 D2
Pape Clément 70 A3
Pape, le 71 G7
Papeterie, la 101 C6
Paradis, du 101 G7
Pardaillan 128 D2
Parsac 101 D8
Partarieu 83 G10
Patâche 115 D8
Patache d'Aux 2 D3
Paveil-de-Luze 54 H5
Pavie 101 E6, 106 G5
Pavie-Décesse 106 G5
Pavie-Macquin 106 G5

Pedesclaux 43 D9
Peillan, le 101 G7
Peillon-Claverie 83 I10
Perenne 128 C2
Pernaud 83 C8
Perrière, la 101 B9
Perron 100 B5, 115 B8
Perruchon 101 B9
Petit Bigaroux 101 F6
Petit Faurie de Soutard
  107 E6
Petit Gravet 101 F6
Petits Arnauds, les 128 D3
Petit-Village 100 C4, 115 G9
Pétrus 100 C5, 115 F9
Peychaud 128 F4
Peyguilhem 100 B2
Peymartin 49 B5
Peyrabon 42 E4
Peyredoulle 128 E3
Peyre-Lebade 54 G2
Peyron 83 H10
Peyroutas 101 G6
Pez, de 37 F7
Phélan Ségur 37 E9
Piada 83 C8
Pibran 43 E8
Picard 37 F8
Pichon-Longueville (Baron)
  43 H9, 49 A5
Pichon-Longueville-
  Comtesse-de-Lalande
  43 I9, 49 A5
Pick, de 83 C9
Pierre-Bibian 54 G1
Pierreière, la 101 E10
Pinet 128 E3
Pin, le 115 G8
Piot 83 C8
Pipeau, Fronsac 100 C1
Pipeau, St-Laurent 101 F7
Plagnac 2 D3
Plain Point 100 B1
Plaisance 101 C6
Plantes, les 83 A8
Plantey, le 3 F6
Plantier-Rose 37 F7
Platanes, des 101 F8
Pleytegeat 83 F9
Plince 115 G7
Pointe, la 115 G7
Pomys 37 G8
Pontac-Lynch 61 B6
Pontac-Monplaisir 71 E8
Pont de Langon, du 71 E8
Pont de Pierre 101 A8
Pontet-Canet 43 E8
Pontet-Clauzure 106 F5
Pontoise-Cabarrus 37 C7
Pontus 100 C2
Potensac 2 G5
Pouget 61 C6
Poujeaux 54 F4
Poumey 70 E5
Poupille 101 F10
Pressac, de 101 F8
Preuillac 2 G3
Prieuré-Lichiné 61 C6
Prost 83 A8
Puy Arnaud 101 F10
Puy-Blanquet Carrille 101 E8
Puy-Castéra 37 H6
Puy, le 101 D8
Queyron 101 F6
Quinault 100 E3
Rabaud-Promis 83 F7
Ramage la Batisse 42 D4
Rasclet 101 G6
Rauzan-Ségla 60 B5
Raux, du 54 C5
Rauzan-Gassies 60 B5
Raymond-Lafon 83 G8
Rayne-Vigneau 83 G7

Remparts, les 83 E8
Rétout, du 54 D5
Rêve d'Or 115 E7
Reysson 36 F4
Richards, les 128 F5
Richelieu 100 D2
Rieussec 83 H9
Rigaillou 71 F7
Rigaud 101 D8
Ripeau 100 D5, 106 C3
Rivereau 128 F5
Rivière, de la 100 B1
Robin 101 E8
Roc de Boissac, du 101 C9
Roc de Joanin 101 D10
Rochemorin 71 H8
Rocher Bellevue 101 G9
Rocher-Corbin 101 B7
Rochers, des 83 C10
Rocheyron 101 E7
Roland 37 I9, 43 C8
Rolland 83 B9
Romer-du-Hayot 83 F10
Roques, de 101 B9
Roudier 101 D7
Rouet 100 B1
Rouget 115 E9
Roumieu 83 C8
Rousselle 128 F2
Rousset 128 G4
Rozier 101 F7
Ruat Petit-Poujeaux 54 H2
St-Amand 83 C9
St-André 101 C7
St-André Corbin 101 C6
St-Bonnet 3 D6
St-Estèphe 37 G7
St-Georges 101 D7
St-Georges Côte Pavie
  106 G5
St-Georges Macquin 101 D6
St-Germain 128 E3
St-Jean de Baron 101 G9
St-Paul 37 D7
St-Philippe, de 101 D10
St-Pierre 48 D6, 54 A4
St-Saturnin 2 D3
St-Vincent 100 B1
Sales, de 100 C4, 115 D6
Salle, la 128 B2
Sanctuaire, le 101 C10
Sansonnet 107 F6
Saransot-du-Pré 54 F2
Segonzac 128 C1
Semeillan-Mazeau 54 H1
Serre, la 106 F5
Siaurac 101 C6
Sigalas-Rabaud 83 G7
Signat 100 B1
Sigognac 3 E6
Simon 83 B8
Sipian 2 G2
Siran 61 C8
Smith Haut-Lafitte 71 G8
Sociando-Mallet 37 C8
Soucarde 128 H4
Soudars 37 A7
Soutard 101 E6, 106 E5
Suau 83 B9
Suduiraut 83 F8
Tailhas, du 106 D1, 115 I8
Taillefer 100 D4, 115 I7
Talbot 49 C5
Tayac, Bourg 128 H3
Tayac, Soussans 55 H6
Temple, le 2 B2
Terrefort 61 D7
Terrey-Gros-Cailloux 48 D6
Tertre-Daugay 106 G3
Tertre, de 60 E5
Tessendey 100 B2
Teynac 48 D6
Teyssier 101 G6

Teyssier, le 101 C8
Thau, de 128 F2
Touilla 83 F10
Toumalin 100 C2
Tourans 101 E8
Tour Bigorre 101 E9
Tour Blanche, la, Bas-Médoc
  3 D6
Tour-Blanche, la, Sauternes
  83 H6
Tour-Carnet, la 49 D3
Tour de By, la 2 B5
Tour de Grenet 101 B8
Tour de Marbuzet 37 G9
Tour-de-Mons, la 55 H7
Tour-de-Pez, La 37 F6
Tour de Ségur, la 101 A8
Tour des Termes 37 E7
Tour d'Horable 101 G10
Tour du Haut Moulin
  54 D5
Tour du Mirail, la 36 H4
Tour du Pin Figeac, la
  100 D5, 106 C2, 115 G9
Tour-du-Roc 54 G5
Tour-Figeac, la 106 D1,
  115 H9
Tour Fonrazade 106 F2
Tour Haut-Caussan 2 F4
Tour Léognan, la 71 F7
Tour Pibran, la 43 E8
Tour-Prignac, la 2 F2
Tour St-Bonnet, la 2 C5
Tour St-Joseph 36 I5
Tours, des 101 C7
Tour Seran, la 2 C5
Tournefeuille 100 C5,
  115 E10
Tourteran 42 E4
Tramont 54 G5
Trapaud 101 F8
Treille des Girondins, la
  101 G9
Trimoulet 101 D6, 107 D6
Trois Moulins 106 F4
Tronquoy-Lalande 37 F8
Troplong-Mondot 107 G6
Trotanoy 100 C4, 115 F8
Trotte Vieille 101 E7,
  107 F6
Tuilerie, la 128 E3
Tuilière, la 128 F3
Valade, la 100 B2
Valoux 71 F9
Verdet 100 E4
Verdignan 37 B7
Vernon 101 D10
Vernous 2 G2
Vésinerie 101 D9
Veyrac 101 E8
Viaud, de 100 B4, 115 B7
Victoria 37 G6
Videlot 100 E3
Vieux Château Certan
  100 C5, 115 F9
Vieux Château Cloquet
  115 E7
Vieux-Château-Landon
  2 D4
Vieux Chênes, des 101 B7
Vieux Chevrol 100 B5,
  115 D10
Villars 100 B2
Villegeorge 54 I5
Villemaurine 106 F5
Vincent 61 B6
Violette, la 115 F8
Vrai-Canon-Bouché 100 D1
Vrai-Canon-Boyer 100 C1
Vray-Croix-de-Gay 115 F9
Yon 101 C7
Yon-Figeac 100 D5, 106 E3
Yquem, d' 83 G8

GAZETTEER

INDEX

Indexer's note: Names of vineyards and wines are often the same and are indexed together eg Ausone, Château 107, 108, 113 where 107, 108 refers to vineyard and 113 to wine. Towns are given in brackets for hotels and restaurants.

INDEX

INDEX

PICTURE CREDITS

Front cover **Scope/Jean Luc Barde**
Back cover **Scope/Jean Luc Barde**

Jason Lowe 5, 16/17, 17, 20 bottom, 23 bottom, 24 bottom, 32 bottom, 32 top, 34 bottom, 38 top, 44 bottom, 44 top, 52 top, 56, 63 centre, 66 bottom, 66/67 top, 68 top left, 68/69 top, 69 bottom, 78 top, 80/81 bottom, 80 left, 84 bottom, 86 bottom, 88/89, 95, 97 top, 102 bottom, 103 bottom, 105 top, 107, 108, 109, 112, 114, 117 top, 118 top, 122, 123, 124/125 top, 130/131, 131, 132, 133, 134/135 top, 135 bottom.
Richard McConnell 27 top right, 82, 117 centre.
Mitchell Beazley/Richard McConnell 30 bottom, 30/31 top, 33, 65 top, 67 top, 110/111.
Scope/Jean Luc Barde 25, 38/39 bottom, 68 bottom, 71 top right, 85, 94, 96/97 bottom, 96 top, 104 top, 113 top, 116/117 bottom, 118/119 bottom, 119 top, 120 top left, /**Michel Guillard** 2, 3, 7, 8/9, 9 top right, 10/11, 12/13, 12, 13, 14, 14/15, 15, 18/19, 20/21 top, 21 top right, 22 centre, 22 bottom, 23 top, 24 top, 26/27, 31 bottom, 34 top left, 34/35 top, 36, 39 top, 40 bottom, 40/41 top, 41 bottom, 42, 45, 46/47, 46, 48/49, 50 top, 50/51 bottom, 51 top, 52 bottom, 53, 57, 58/59 bottom, 59 top, 60, 62, 63 top, 63 bottom, 64/65 bottom, 70/71, 74, 75, 76, 78 top, 79, 84 top, 86/87 top, 89 right, 90/91, 92, 93, 98/99, 99 top right, 102/103 top, 104/105, 113 bottom, 120 bottom, 120/121 top, 125 top, 126/127, 127 top right, 129, 134 top left, /**Jean Daniel Sudres** 22 top.